KEROUAC IN FLORIDA

Where the Road Ends

by Bob Kealing
Foreword by David Amram

WITH BEST WISHES,
Bob Kealing

ARBITER PRESS
ORLANDO · NEW YORK

A R B I T E R   P R E S S
O R L A N D O • N E W Y O R K

Quotes by Jack Kerouac have been printed with original punctuation and word usage.

Passages from Kerouac's writing reprinted by permission of Sterling Lord Literistic, Inc. Copyright by Jack Kerouac.

Kerouac Photo Gallery courtesy of Fred DeWitt and the Orange County Regional History Center.

Photographic scans courtesy of Florida Imaging, 5125 Adanson St., Suite 200, Orlando, FL 32804

A portion of the proceeds from the sale of this book will benefit the Jack Kerouac Writers-in-Residence Project of Orlando, a nonprofit 501(c)(3) charity.

Editor: Erin West
Copy Editor: Bonnie Fesmire
Editorial Coordinator: Christine Blackwell
Art Director: Alicia Ziff
Compositor: Carolyn Boyle

Library of Congress Control Number: 2003113868

ISBN: 0-9621385-3-3

10 9 8 7 6 5 4 3 2 1

For Karen, William and Kristen
with love

In memory of
David Bloom,
former colleague and friend

Acknowledgments

The author would like to thank John Sampas and the Estate of Jack and Stella Kerouac for their generosity during the research for this book.

The author would also like to thank Christine Blackwell for her invaluable mentoring during this process. Editor Erin Styers West added focus and enthusiasm when it was needed. Thanks to Bonnie Fesmire for her unfailing attention to detail. Thanks to Alicia Ziff for her visual artistry and willingness to roll with the myriad changes.

A special thanks to Marty Cummins who, along with his wife, Jan, came up with the idea for a living, literary tribute to Jack Kerouac in Florida and spent countless hours and days making that dream come true. What an amazing journey it has become.

Thanks to members of the Kerouac Project board: Grace and Fred Hagedorn, Nancy Granger, Yvonne David, Jodi Rubin and Mark Schenkel, Summer Rodman, Keith and Monica Lochmandy, Loren Ford, Bruce Gordy, Sam Hill, Charlie Sum, Richard Frolich, Maureen Morell, Carolyn Miller, Nancy Hanniford, Al Chiodi, Ormund Powers, Karen Good, Jackson Walker, Stuart Omans, Maurice O'Sullivan, Phil Deaver, Mark Garrett, Brad Kuhn, Kathy Lightcap, and all the others who volunteered their time to make the project a reality. Thanks to Annie O'Neill, Les Anderson, and Lauri Mahlmberg. Thanks to Lenny Roland. Thanks to Annette King and Robin Chapman. Thanks to Joe Brooks and his photographic artistry. Thanks to David Watson, design consultant, and to Bob Sheridan and Florida Imaging, who provided the photo scans. Thanks to Letty Marques. Thanks to Jonathan Harrington in the New York office. Thanks to a most generous benefactor, Jeffrey Cole. Thanks to Darden Restaurants for their financial generosity to the Kerouac Project.

Special thanks to David Amram for his positive energy, his belief in the Kerouac Project, and his willingness to share friendship and find the good. Thanks to Carolyn Cassady for enduring the humidity. Thanks to Dan Wakefield for his support. Thanks to Helen Weaver for sharing her memories.

Thanks to the present and past Floridians who've been Jack, Stella, and Gabrielle Kerouac's friends and neighbors. Many weren't looking for attention but saw enough relevance in what the author was doing to share their memories: Eleanore Feller, Carol and John Ney, Fred DeWitt, Audrey and Dave Redding, Paul Gleason, Jean Yothers, Kenny Sears, Ron Lowe, Nell and Cheryl Burrow, Betty Whatley, Midge Laughlin, and Anne Houston.

For their support and encouragement, gratitude is due to John K. Kealing, Jane Kealing, William L. Kealing, friends at WESH-TV, and the Orange County Regional History Center.

And thanks to all the artists who've been guests at the Kerouac House. May your time there continue to provide inspiration for years to come.

Contents

Foreword

Soon after Jack Kerouac and I began collaborating, he told me about his happy and productive times when he would stay with his sister, Caroline, in Orlando.

In early January of 1957, Jack came by the Five Spot in New York City from Orlando. I had just started playing there with my quartet. I invited him to read some of his work with our group accompanying him. Later that night, we talked until dawn, as we often did. Our topic was Jack's ability to write when he stayed in Florida and the South. We talked about how the spirit of Cabeza de Vaca still resonated in the air of those incredible late-night, early-morning hours, and how the Seminole Indians have kept their connection to ancient times as part of their secret to maintaining their way of life. Jack made vivid how all of this gave a special feeling when he was creating alone in the silence of a Southern night.

Soon afterwards, having signed his Viking contract for *On the Road*, Kerouac took off on a freighter for one of his many journeys.

Even then, Florida was one of his ports of call. However, those quiet days were about to end.

After *On the Road* was published in September of 1957, Jack's world changed forever. Florida, like his hometown of Lowell, became a place of refuge, shielding him from the enormous glare of unsolicited and unwanted publicity, followed a short time later by an avalanche of critical savagery. When Jack bought himself and his mother a house in Northport, Long Island, it reminded him of his beloved Lowell.

When Jack finally returned to Florida, the perception among the literary cognoscenti was that he was finished as a writer.

"How can you say that?" I asked a well-known editor at a literary gathering in the early 1960s in New York City. "Why is it," I asked, "that so many presumably educated people think that every place south of New Jersey is inhabited by illiterate morons who don't wear shoes and don't read books? How about the fact that many of our greatest writers still come from the South?"

"Yes, David, you have a point," the editor said gently, "but none of them who had any kind of major career would ever choose . . . *Florida*. After all, Florida is where people go to die."

Bob Kealing's new book is the first written account of Kerouac's years spent in the state he chose to make his home so that he and his mother could have a place to *live*.

Kealing's own background as an Emmy Award-winning television journalist gives him the eye and ear for detail and the ability to tell a story in a way that puts you in the middle of it. His exceptional ability to interview people who would usually be hesitant to share their feelings gives this extraordinary book the authentic feel for the kinds of people, places, events, sights, and sounds that Kerouac himself wrote about—neighbors, friends, people who never read Kerouac's work but knew him as a person. Musicians, fellow artists, and people from all walks of life tell us about the Jack Kerouac they knew.

Using primary sources, Kealing traces a story that rivals the best ones told by Kerouac himself. Like Kerouac's legacy, the story continues after his death and through the beginning of the new millennium. Kealing examines the amazing renaissance of Kerouac's work and tells the story of the run-down, roach-infested house in Orlando that he and Marty Cummins helped to become The Kerouac Writers' Residence.

Jack began his career as a sports writer for his hometown paper, the *Lowell Sun*.

"You've always got to tell a story, Davey," Kerouac often said to me. "Just like music, no matter how abstract it gets, you've got to tell a story."

"You always manage to do that, Jack," I said. "Someday, all the naysayers are going to see that you were the reporter of our era."

Now, Bob Kealing's new book makes him our reporter of *this* era. The few of us left from our era who knew and worked with Jack will always be grateful that this story of Jack's years in Florida has finally been told in such a compelling and truthful way.

Bob Kealing is a true journalist. He tells the story in an honest, often touching, and uncompromising way that Jack himself would have loved.

—David Amram, Putnam Valley, New York

(David Amram worked with Jack Kerouac as his principal musical collaborator from 1956 until Kerouac's death in 1969. They gave the first-ever jazz/poetry readings together in New York City in October 1957, collaborated on the historic film Pull My Daisy *in 1959, worked on the cantata* A Year in Our Land, *and remained friends for life. Amram has continued working on Kerouac's behalf to the present day. In 2002 Thunder's Mouth Press published Amram's* Offbeat: Collaborating with Kerouac. *Amram continues to compose symphonic music and tour the world as a composer/conductor/multi-instrumentalist.)*

Introduction

I have another novel in mind—"On the Road"—which I
keep thinking about;—About two guys hitch-hiking
to California in search of something they don't really
find, and losing themselves on the road, and coming
all the way back hopeful of something else.

Jack Kerouac
July 28, 1948

It took a trip to one of the busiest urban areas in the world, New York City, to begin this story of Jack Kerouac's life in Florida. And I don't mind telling you, some kind of fibrillation pulsed through my chest when the library curator plunked down four gray, rectangular boxes in front of me, marked *18 a, b, c,* and *d.* I'd submersed myself in this project for months, and this was a key moment. I opened 18a and found a hodge-podge of spiral stenographer's notebooks. The worn, decades-old paper had yellowed, and the pencilled words were legible but ghostly.

The notebooks comprised Jack Kerouac's prose and "pomes," his dreams and doodling, partial and complete manuscripts written in notebooks small enough to fit in his shirt pocket. The notebooks and journals spanned his life, beginning with his childhood in Massachusetts. There were also letters to friends and family, thoughts written down seemingly as they had entered his mind. Many of the letters and postcards were in the classic Kerouac single-spaced type. I noticed quite a few with postmarks from Orlando and St. Petersburg.

Kerouac made it clear he meant to have these words read. Before me was a good chunk of the life story he liked to call his "Legend of Duluoz." Kerouac monkeyed around with the names and such, but what he was actually doing was turning his life into literature. Everything he thought seemed to go down on paper, even if those thoughts might potentially bring him embarrassment. No matter. It was as Kerouac himself had written, "What a man most wishes to hide, revise, and unsay, is precisely what Literature is waiting and bleeding for."

Words. Kerouac's crucible for existence. His record of the most mundane or wrenching moments of his life. The sheer amount of words and the intensity of the writing are at times astonishing. Thank God there were no word processors in those days, no laptops with which to capture all these words, thoughts, and feelings on some impotent diskette. The handwriting often gives an immediate insight into Kerouac's state of mind. Sometimes the words roll smoothly and effortlessly in the manuscripts: "Neal and I are in Mexico City buying weed off a bunch of Mexican court-dancer queers." Other times, the writing is large and

Jack Kerouac's notebooks at the Berg Collection, New York Public Library.

exaggerated, suggesting Kerouac was angry or drunk: "To a critic: Thanks a lot for your overwhelming scholarly insight into your own envy."

In addition to notebooks and letters, I found travel logs, budgets, and grocery lists, all recorded fastidiously with the passion of a man for his mistress. There were discharge papers from the Merchant Marines and a library card from St. Petersburg showing a portly, middle-aged Kerouac. I looked at a clipping from the *Lowell Sun* about a touchdown Kerouac scored in a big high-school football game.

For years this material was locked away and unavailable. After Kerouac's death, his last wife put it all away. She'd try to deal with it at some other time, or someone else would. She had her reasons.

It was worth a couple of thousand-mile trips for insight into Kerouac's life in Florida. Decades fell away, and faded words on old papers came alive. One letter was written on Pabst Blue Ribbon stationery, and at the bottom, *May we suggest Pabst Blue Ribbon with your next meal?* Another was a heartbreaking missive Kerouac wrote to his fallen friend and soul mate, Sebastian Sampas. Upon news of Sampas' death in World

War II, in a state of desperate sadness Kerouac wrote, "It's raining—and the song has come—I'll see you again. Where? Where, Sammy?"

Like no one I've ever read, Jack Kerouac evokes the romantic notions of America so many of us possess but find hard to put into words. At the same time, Kerouac expresses the yearning and sadness we all know due to the limitations of our lives. It is that bittersweet combination that is so appealing, so common-man, so honest, so Jack Kerouac. And in that sense, generation after generation, his work continues to stir the soul of America—and the world.

Over and over during the last twelve years of his life, Jack Kerouac followed the road to central Florida. Kerouac endured personal struggles here that he rarely wrote about publicly. And little-known friends and neighbors who witnessed his struggles recount their stories now. To the unaware, the homes and neighborhoods where it all played out resemble countless others dotting Florida's sun-drenched landscape.

Kerouac's writings, new interviews with friends and neighbors, and many books written by and about Kerouac provided the road map for this journey.

ORLANDO

1956–1962

Orlando, Florida - Azalea Blossom Time

Yates Street

December 1956–July 1957

So therefore I dedicate myself to myself, to my art, my sleep, my dreams, my labors, my suffrances, my loneliness, my unique madness, my endless absorption and hunger— because I cannot dedicate myself to any fellow being.

Jack Kerouac

My car crept along until I spotted the address, written in black like a signature above the carport: 1219 Yates Street, the home where Jack Kerouac stayed during his first visit to Orlando. Above the doorbell of this single-story block home was a line of masking tape and instructions to do something; I couldn't make out what. Just then an older woman's voice cooed, "Hello . . . over here."

"Where?" I asked myself.

Finally my eyes caught a small rectangular opening cut from the door of the finished garage. Through the screen, an older woman peered out at me, then swung open the door. The garage had been transformed into a cozy TV room. Eleanore Feller allowed me into her home, and I told her about my journey.

"You know, some people from Rollins College have been here a few times asking about him," Eleanore offered, sitting in a comfortable chair. "But I don't know much. Some writer, a real wild man."

Some writer indeed.

Jack Kerouac arrived at the Winter Park bus station just outside Orlando in December 1956. At the time few knew of the thirty-four-year-old writer. He'd published only one novel, *The Town and the City*. He had used the name John Kerouac with that book. Critical response was polite but tepid. No matter, he pursued what he saw as his life's work with an undying fervor. That pursuit meant traveling thousands of miles, recording his impressions of the scenes he saw and the characters he met along the way. He studied people and took special care to remember the language they used, the way they talked.

Kerouac had taken and written about many of his great journeys before he blew into Orlando in 1956. During his publishing drought, he had chiseled out eleven books of prose and poetry. By the time he was thirty-two, Kerouac, by his own estimate, had written a million and a half words, many in longhand. Along the way he'd been a hobo, railroad brakeman, merchant seaman, and panhandler. But these experiences were grist for his autobiographical novels. All that work at writing was about to pay off in ways he could never have imagined. What would turn out to be Kerouac's most famous book was about to be published.

For years publishers had rejected *On the Road* as unwieldy and impossible to revise, but Viking's Malcolm Cowley had been interested in the unorthodox work since 1953. In his acceptance report, Cowley envisioned *On the Road* as a work that would stand for a long time. He called the book "the honest record of another way of life." However, Cowley was concerned about libel, so he asked Kerouac to change the names of the people he had written about. That would be one of Kerouac's projects upon arrival at his sister Caroline's new home in the Orlando suburbs.

In the 1950s, the land boom and aerospace explosion brought thousands of ambitious new residents to central Florida. The success of the Russian satellite *Sputnik* fueled the space race to a frenzy. On the eastern coast, Florida began to come alive with engineers and scientists transforming the sleepy expanse into the space coast. Florida's vast, flat tracts of land offered spacious runways for those in the military and aircraft industries. At the same time, modern highways made car travel easy and practical for the middle class. Orlando was ripe for the transformation from an agrarian economy to one based on tourism and technology.

All of this came as promising news to Jack Kerouac's brother-in-law, Paul Blake. Blake, a former military airman based in Rocky Mount, North Carolina, was looking for a way to cash in on the American space race. For a man with his ambitions, a rural stretch of the Carolinas was nowhere. He had limited success in a television repair and installation business. When an old military buddy in the Civil Air Patrol wrote to Blake about all Orlando had to offer, he soon made up his mind. Blake, his wife Caroline, and son Paul Jr. would be like the legions of others heading south to pursue the good life in central Florida.

Caroline Kerouac met Paul Blake during World War II. She was in the Women's Air Corps; he flew for the U.S. Air Force. Devoutly Catholic, Caroline had been married once before but had the union annulled, the only proper way for someone of her faith to get out of a lifelong commitment. The two married not long after the end of the war. To fulfill their role in America's postwar population boom, Caroline became pregnant with twins. Soon, however, doctors discovered that Caroline had toxemia—a potentially life-threatening complication. On June 10, 1948, doctors performed an emergency C-section. Paul Jr. survived, but a second boy, Peter, was stillborn.

To help out, Caroline's and Jack's mother, Gabrielle, came to stay with the Blakes. After Paul Jr.'s birth, her nickname became "Memere," French for Grandma. Jack also became a fixture at the Blake household in North Carolina. When the Blakes decided to move south, Memere went with them. And where Memere went, her twice-divorced son would soon follow. In the fall of 1956, the Blakes rented a small place in a northwest Orlando neighborhood known as College Park. Memere made the trip by car with them.

The week before Christmas 1956, Kerouac arrived at his sister's Orlando home and reflected on all that had transpired in the months and years before. As he later wrote in *Desolation Angels*, "On the porch of the house was my old rolltop desk with all the unpublished manuscripts in it, and the couch where I slept. To sit at my desk and stare was sad. All the work I'd done at it, four novels and innumerable dreams and poems and notes."

Kerouac wore blue jeans and a wrinkled shirt, long before the craze caught on. He often carried a small notebook in his front pocket. "You'd be talking about something," one neighbor remembered, "and he'd be staring at you, and all of a sudden he'd turn around, pick up his pad and write something down."

This unusual behavior created tensions between Jack and Paul Blake. The two men couldn't have been more different. To a military man like Blake, Kerouac's nomadic and introspective ways seemed frivolous and immature; writing in no way seemed to be a secure way to make a living. For his part, Kerouac didn't like loud and bossy types like Blake. Kerouac had left the Columbia University football team due to clashes with his coach. His brief military record reflected the same kind of rebellion against authority. Kerouac translated his attitude into literature, and an American cultural revolution would soon be born. But had it not been for Memere's willingness to give the Blakes money, Kerouac could have found himself without a place to call home between his wanderings.

Whatever problems Jack and Paul Sr. had did not inhibit Jack's relationship with Paul Jr. Shortly after Jack arrived in Florida, he and eight-year-old Paul headed off on bicycles to buy an Elvis Presley record. Young Paul so idolized the new southern singing sensation that he used to hold a banjo, close his eyes, and do a dead-on impression of him. Just a year before, in July of 1955, twenty-year-old Presley blew away a capacity crowd at Orlando's Municipal Auditorium when he opened the show for another rising star, Andy Griffith.

When Presley returned to Orlando in August of 1956, a Jacksonville judge admonished that Presley's swiveling hips amounted to "an obscene burlesque dance." But if Presley pushed the envelope, the Beats were about to set it on fire. The book that would make Kerouac famous the next year dealt with taboo subjects like drifting, drunkenness, and casual sex. But it also challenged many of the rigid, stereotypical conceptions of life in post–World War II America. And it challenged those who lived that life—like Paul Blake Sr.

On Christmas Eve, Kerouac, Memere, and the Blakes sat in front of the television and sipped martinis. Thanks to TV they could watch mass as it happened in New York City. Midnight mass had always been a tradition for the Kerouacs, and as soon as Jack and his sister were old enough to stay up late, they were allowed to attend midnight services in their hometown of Lowell, Massachusetts. Kerouac wrote about "parties of people laughing down the street, bright throbbing stars of New England winter bending over rooftops sometimes causing long rows of icicles to shimmer as we passed." Years later, during Christmas of 1956, it was Memere who couldn't stay awake. Jack pulled out his notepad and sketched his mother as she slept.

Thanks to Kerouac's meticulous record-keeping, he retained copies of most of his letters. Those letters he wrote from Yates Street reveal a writer still very much in love with his craft. Indeed, the subject of writing, editing, and publishing occupied much of his correspondence. Despite any premonitions about how dreary fame would be, Kerouac was thrilled that another of his books would be published. He could show his brother-in-law that he was no joke, that intelligent people knew to take Jack Kerouac's writing seriously. And then there was the matter of a New York love interest.

On the last Saturday of '56, Kerouac wrote a full-page letter addressed to his "sweetheart," Helen Weaver, nine years his junior. Kerouac and his poet friend Allen Ginsberg had met Weaver's roommate, and on one cold November evening they appeared below the women's snowy New York City window. As Weaver and Kerouac became acquainted and argued about Thomas Wolfe and Henry James, the two fell madly and instantaneously in love. Now Kerouac was a thousand miles away, lovesick.

In a seductive tone, Kerouac wrote that he thought about Weaver in bed at night, "what I'd do to you if I had you there." Their time together in New York was still fresh in his mind, "dancing, singing, getting up in the morning," he recalled. "I have another week here, of mad typing and working on FOUR different manuscripts, that'll make us rich." At the end of that time, Kerouac planned to return to New York and Weaver, to celebrate his first book deal in years. "I'll be there, in my new clothes," Kerouac told her. "And I hope you'll like to see me there . . . And I'll kiss you . . . your soft lips." He signed the letter "Jean (who loves you)."

The day after Christmas, Kerouac wrote to Allen Ginsberg about plans for a trip to Tangier. The same day, Kerouac told his editor, Keith Jennison, that he would have to "demand" that his forthcoming book be titled *On the Road*, not *Anywhere Road* as Viking had suggested. "It is the DEFINITE road of beatness," Kerouac wrote. "Anywhere Road sounds like the opposite idea." Kerouac assured his editors that he was continuing to trim his manuscript of any libelous touches. He was indeed working hard. He commented to Weaver, "Tho I'm supposed to be a lazy bum, I haven't done anything for the last twelve days but rattle this typewriter day and night tryna catch up with my wild manuscripts."

The second week in January, Kerouac readied himself for the trip to New York. He planned to bring much of his prodigious output over the last few years with him, hoping that Viking would be interested in publishing more of his work. In one big, double-handled suitcase Kerouac stashed a half dozen manuscripts: *Visions of Neal, Desolation Angels, Book of Blues, Book of Dreams, Some of the Dharma,* and *Tristessa.*

The anticipated New York reunion with Helen Weaver that Kerouac had written about so hotly and heavily proved short-lived. Free from the stifling confines of his mother, the Blakes, and suburban Orlando, Kerouac's celebration of his new book deal never ended. For two weeks, Kerouac drank himself into oblivion and invited his friends to sleep on Weaver's floor. One morning Helen kicked Jack out.

Fresh from the ashes of his short but passionate relationship with Helen Weaver, Kerouac needed a place to crash. To help his friend, Ginsberg facilitated a blind date for him with a twenty-one-year-old aspiring novelist named Joyce Glassman. Although they did not spend a great deal of time together, it was this relationship that lasted through the rest of a tumultuous year. Glassman was instrumental in documenting the couple's emotional journey through the rough waters ahead.

Although she knew of Kerouac only by description, Glassman's first sight of him was a revelation. She has written of her relationship with Kerouac under her married name, Joyce Johnson. "He totally charmed me when I met him," Johnson recalled. "He had a kind of sweetness and melancholy about him that were both very appealing." That first night she bought Kerouac frankfurters, home fries, and baked beans. The two began to share her apartment.

In March, Kerouac left New York for a wandering journey to Morocco and France. In Tangier, he helped writer William S. Burroughs with what would become Burroughs' classic Beat primer, *Naked Lunch*. A bad drug trip caused Kerouac to fall ill, but he continued on to France. There he hitched rides through the countryside, stopping to sketch the scenery. He yearned to learn more about the roots of his French ancestry.

In April, Kerouac returned to the Blakes' home in Orlando, but only long enough to get his belongings ready for yet another long journey. For some time, he had dreamed of going to California to live with two people he loved, Neal and Carolyn Cassady. Jack promised his mother they would live near the Cassadys and eat big Sunday dinners together. Jack wrote to Carolyn Cassady, "I'm praying now that I'll finally make it to my true home." He also wrote to Neal, informing him that *On the Road* would be published in the fall. Jack had made Neal the main character in the book, under the name Dean Moriarty; and he commented with some concern, "I sure do hope no one recognizes you too much in that opus."

As they had done so often, Kerouac and his mother gathered their scattered belongings for a long journey. He was not looking forward to traveling that far. "There's hardly anything in the world or at least America more miserable than a transcontinental bus trip with limited means " Not to mention with your sixty-two-year-old mother. Kerouac described that trip in Book Two of *Desolation Angels*:

> It's hot in May in Florida—I long to get out and go west
> beyond the East Texas Plain to that High Plateau and on
> over the Divide to dry Arizonies and beyond—Poor Ma is
> standing there absolutely dependent on me . . .

On May 6, 1957, like a couple of Dust Bowl Okies, the inseparable mother and son boarded a bus for California. Over the throngs of citrus groves still ranging the central Florida landscape, they headed north, "towards the panhandle Tallahassees and Mobile Alabamas of morning, no prospect of New Orleans till noon and already fair exhausted." Kerouac obviously felt a strong sense of guilt for dragging his aging mother this far. "Sometimes during the night I'd look at my poor sleeping mother cruelly *crucified* there in the American night because of no-money, no-hope-of-money, no family, no nothing."

The Cassadys, meanwhile, did not know that Jack and his mother were on the way. Carolyn Cassady later revealed in her book *Off the Road* that she was shocked to get a postcard from Kerouac mailed from Berkeley. Neal went to Berkeley to see Jack, who gave him an advance copy of *On the Road*. Carolyn had expected that Jack would soon come to the Cassadys' home in Los Gatos, which was some distance away. She looked forward to a grand reunion with Jack. Years earlier, she and Jack had had a love affair while he stayed in the Cassadys' home.

Despite the obvious passion and kinship between her and Jack, Carolyn's big reunion with him and her chance to meet Memere never happened. After what Jack described as one "little ole earth quake," Memere had had enough. "California is sinister," she declared. "I wanta spend my social security checks in Florida." The pull of Caroline and her little grandson was too strong for Memere, and those checks were crucial. At the time, Jack and his mother had a combined income of less than $200 a month.

As quickly as Jack and Memere moved to California, they were headed right back to Orlando. "He never brought her down here—or contacted me at all," Cassady lamented in *Off the Road*. "But Neal was unable to explain it. I was very hurt. It was an episode never unraveled between Jack and me."

Jack rationalized the move in a letter to poet Gary Snyder. "I remember and realize the horror of this place with its TOO MANY COPS AND TOO MANY LAWS and general killjoy culture." Despite Jack's grand pronouncements and protestations, this was a move to make his mother happy. It's what consumed Jack's life after this point, keeping Memere happy, caring for Memere, and having Memere cook and clean for him as she always did.

July Fourth came and went in Berkeley, and days later the Kerouacs were on their way back east. But it would be humiliating to be back in the Blakes' home for long. Jack knew Big Paul would see this as just another example of his laughable rootlessness. Only this time he had subjected his mother to a grueling journey, and all for what? Jack needed to find a place for Memere close to the Blakes so he could get back on his own road, and back to writing. Jack and Memere rode the Greyhound bus all that miserable way back to College Park.

That ended Kerouac's association with the house Eleanore Feller calls home. I was ready for the next piece of my own sleuthing through the summer suburbs of Kerouac's 1957. "You know, he lived right down the street with his mother somewhere." Feller's sweet, small voice confirmed some of the clues I'd already gotten. Now I was off to find the small apartment Kerouac rented for Memere upon their return from California. It turned out to be the least known and most historically sig-nificant of all the places Kerouac called home during his life in Florida. At first, finding it proved to be as difficult as Kerouac's search for a home during that restless stretch.

1418^{1/2} Clouser Avenue

July 1957–April 1958

And this is the way a novel gets written, in ignorance, fear, sorrow, madness, and a kind of psychotic happiness that serves as an incubator for the wonders being born.

Jack Kerouac

The little place that Kerouac shared with his mother the summer of 1957 had been talked about in College Park for years, but no one seemed sure of its exact location. Weeks went by. Finally I made a phone call to the executor of Kerouac's estate, his brother-in-law, John Sampas.

"It says here 1418 and a half Cloiser Street," Sampas said in a rich Bostonian accent. Kerouac had made a list of all the places he lived. Sampas was kind enough to read it to me and solve the mystery.

1418½ Clouser Avenue sits just around the corner from Caroline Blake's old house on Yates Street. This little Florida Cracker house looks just like the kind of place you might imagine Kerouac calling home. Clouser is really more back alley than avenue. But what the little north-south artery lacks in breadth, it compensates for in charm. Tucked away off the intersection of Clouser and Shady Lane, the single-story wood frame house is situated beneath a glorious live oak. Spanish moss drips from a network of massive, arching branches.

Back from his abbreviated trip to California, his hopes of living with the Cassadys dashed, Kerouac had returned to College Park in Orlando. He spent most of the $45 he had left on renting an apartment for himself and his mother. The little dwelling was a converted back porch. Many such apartments had been added to existing homes to help house all the bachelor soldiers returning from World War II. After the bad experience with drugs in Tangier, then that wasted trek to California, Kerouac thought he might finally be settled.

Kerouac's mother was happy with the place too. There were big shade trees to help deflect the intense Florida heat. In addition, there were nine orange trees, five grapefruit trees, and four more with tangerines. Kerouac's mother told him, "I'll never move again. I'll die right here in paradise." Kerouac felt a sense of security that this could be his winter writing retreat. With his mother happy and close to her family, Kerouac could travel again "conscience free."

Despite his initial excitement, Kerouac was unfamiliar with summer in Florida. Writing to Allen Ginsberg soon after the move, he called the Florida summer a "heatwave horror" and announced that he was leaving for the "cool plateau of Mexico City." Kerouac had other reasons for going to Mexico too. In a letter to his editor at Viking, he wrote that he wanted "complete solitude" for writing. He also explained that being in Mexico would help him finish his latest work-in-progress, *Doctor Sax*, which he had originally written during a stay in Mexico. Returning to Mexico would renew the inspiration he needed to write some extra scenes for the book, which was based on memories of his childhood.

In that same letter, Kerouac asked for an advance from the royalties of *On the Road*. "God knows how much money there'll be for me in September!" Kerouac predicted. He expected the book to sell at least five thousand copies. That would mean another thousand dollars of income, a princely sum for Kerouac at that time. For the time being, Kerouac would head to Mexico broke. He knew this was risky but resolved to go anyway: "I feel the call." However, there was someone else to consider, the sensitive twenty-one-year-old woman he'd left behind.

The night before leaving Orlando, Kerouac wrote Joyce Glassman in New York. He lamented that $33 was all he had left in the world to make another Mexico trek. He was still embarrassed that he'd gone all the way to California with such grandiose plans and ended up back in Orlando, barely two blocks from his sister's home. Caroline and her husband didn't let Jack forget it. "Everybody comes around every night to laugh," Jack complained.

Jack asked Joyce to join him in Mexico in September. That would give him some time alone before her presence could distract him from his writing. Joyce had just received a $500 advance on her own novel-in-progress. "In a year we'll both be rich and corrupt!" Jack joked.

Days after Kerouac's departure, word reached Memere that there had been an earthquake in Mexico City. She worried that she had not heard from her son. She wrote Kerouac's friend Philip Whalen and asked whether he had heard from her "Jacky" and could forward his new address to her. It turned out Kerouac had come through the earthquake without a scratch. After the earthquake, he wrote to Joyce and invited her to come on down to be with him. But his stay in Mexico would be cut short by sickness.

"I GOT ASIATIC FLU," Kerouac wrote Allen Ginsberg from Mexico City. "GOING HOME." Less than three weeks after Kerouac's arrival, and a full week before his girlfriend was scheduled to get on a plane bound for Mexico, he was headed back to Orlando. "I just couldn't sweat it out sick and alone," he wrote to her when he returned.

Kerouac made it back to Orlando by mid-August and took a cab to Clouser Avenue. When Kerouac found Memere wasn't home, he curled up in the grass still sick with fever.

In less than a year, Kerouac had already journeyed to Orlando four times. But this would be his last journey back as a broke and unknown writer. Overcome with fever and lying under the shade of citrus trees in his mother's little back-porch encampment, Kerouac also perched on the precipice of literary immortality. Soon he would board a Greyhound bus for New York City and get caught in a whirlwind of publicity. "He had absolutely no notion of what awaited him," Joyce Johnson remembered.

Joyce was overjoyed that Jack wanted to be in New York for the publication of *On the Road*. Finally one of Jack's journeys would bring him back to her. On August 23, 1957, her letter and a $30 check arrived at 1418 1/2 Clouser Avenue. Immediately Kerouac's spirits lifted. In case of a relapse into his illness, Kerouac decided to wait another week in

Orlando before buying his bus ticket and heading out.

Jack arrived at Joyce's apartment on 68th Street off Central Park just before *On the Road*'s publication, which was set for September 5. At midnight, they ventured out to the newsstand near the subway entrance at 66th and Broadway. Kerouac's book of hyperkinetic travels establishing Dean Moriarty as the American anti-hero was to be reviewed in the morning edition of *The New York Times*.

Gilbert Millstein's write-up was extraordinary. He gushed that *On the Road* was "an authentic work of art" and "a major novel." He called the book's publication historic and compared Kerouac to Hemingway. The review wasn't just establishing Kerouac as an important new writer, it was his coronation as the voice of a new generation.

Fortunately for history's sake, someone with rare sensitivity and insight was there to witness Kerouac's reactions. "He could barely sort of take it in," Johnson remembered. "He kept reading it and shaking his head and saying, 'Well, I think it's pretty good, what do you think?' "

The two returned to Joyce's apartment to go to sleep. By the next morning, the phone started ringing and never stopped. Overnight, Kerouac's life had changed forever. He now belonged to the world.

As King of the Beat Generation, Kerouac was thrust into the spotlight, receiving a kind of scrutiny and attention he could not have imagined riding up to New York on that Greyhound bus. Kerouac wrote to Carolyn Cassady of parties where he was "drunk alatime." He was setting the tone for how he would deal with fame and critics for the rest of his life. Booze loosened up Kerouac enough that he could assume the role of court jester and, perhaps, bon vivant to reporters and other literary types. People expected him to be like Dean Moriarty, the hero of *On the Road*, even though he was really Sal Paradise, the narrator and observer, trying to keep up with friends he described as burning Roman candles.

The truth was that the thirty-five-year-old author, as his letters indicate, was becoming world-weary of rootless travel. Many in the public didn't get it. Kerouac wasn't the same person he was when he wrote *On the Road*, and he had never been the person some of his critics and fans expected him to be. Those critical distinctions became malignant problems in Kerouac's life after the publication of *On the Road*.

Kerouac had become a media darling before people knew what that was. Television was still a new medium, but already its power was becoming evident. Kerouac appeared on one of the first talk shows, *Night Beat*. Interviewers pressed him, *What was this Beat Generation anyway?*

After Millstein, many others dismissed Kerouac's spontaneous-prose style as infantile. Truman Capote's oft-quoted criticism dismissed it as mere "typewriting." Still others found Kerouac's homage to a restless and wayward subculture threatening and un-American. "Neal and I, too, were surprised at the ferocity and cruelty of many of the reviewers," Carolyn Cassady wrote in *Off the Road*. "They were like angry dogs threatened by a wolf." In many places, including Orlando, *On the Road* was very controversial.

Joyce Johnson has described the critical backlash and its effect on the powerfully shy and introspective Kerouac. "I can't think of any American writer who endured such persistent abuse from critics . . . it was very, very devastating for him," Johnson said.

Meanwhile, Kerouac tried to argue that the word *Beat* meant *beatific* and that he and the other people fictionalized in the novel were on a spiritual quest for truth and meaning beyond the rigid confines of 1950s America. No matter how Kerouac's partying days with Neal Cassady were interpreted, they were all but over, and his recent travels in 1956 were about introspection, religion, and spirituality. Nevertheless, 1957 was also the time of McCarthyism, and any excuse to feed that "us versus them" mentality was rarely passed up by moralizing opportunists. Kerouac was a prime target, even though he didn't want to be a political figure or cultural guru. He just wanted to write his books, make some money, gain literary respect, and coexist comfortably with Memere.

Johnson witnessed Kerouac's retreat from fame. "The only way he seemed to get himself through this period was to step up his drinking," Johnson remembered. The man who championed Kerouac's work in the *Times*, Gilbert Millstein, threw a party for him. But Kerouac was so traumatized by all the controversy, adulation, criticism, partying, insults, and hangers-on that he wouldn't leave his girlfriend's apartment.

Kerouac's fifth trip back home to Orlando that year would be an escape. This journey would be about maintaining sanity and hiding out. No matter what happened, he could always return home to Memere. The seven weeks in New York City had been unlike anything Kerouac had ever experienced in his life. Sure, he'd seen another book published before, *The Town and the City*, but *On the Road* catapulted him to another level. The book was selling, and Kerouac finally had some money in his pocket. He could afford to take an $80 train ride home to Orlando.

Kerouac's young girlfriend was once again seeing off the troubled man of her fading dreams. One day in September, Kerouac almost proposed to her but didn't. Their relationship had changed. She later wrote in her memoir that it seemed Kerouac wanted her to be his mother as much as or more than his lover. "I found myself having to take care of Jack to get him through this whole experience," recalled Johnson. The two stopped by a White Castle hamburger stand so Kerouac could stock up for his train trip. Eight burgers would sustain him on the trip back.

It didn't take long for Kerouac to become rejuvenated. From a thousand miles away, in the reassuring anonymity of his mother's tiny lair, fame seemed to suit Kerouac just fine. It would keep him from going stir-crazy in the cramped isolation of his mother's place. In addition, the fame was a long-overdue affirmation to Kerouac's family that maybe there was something to all this writing he'd done. And he was ready to do more. The coming weeks were among the most prolific of Kerouac's later life.

Kerouac's career was starting to boil. There were phone calls from magazines wanting stories. Kerouac's agent, Sterling Lord, said Marlon Brando was interested in bringing *On the Road* to the big screen. Lillian Hellman suggested Kerouac write a play. By mid-October, Kerouac was poised to make history in that little cottage on Clouser Avenue, where, barely two months before, he had collapsed in the yard sick from fever and dead broke. Kerouac's spirits soared with word that *On the Road* was number eleven on the *New York Times* bestseller list. He couldn't wait to show this further validation to his skeptical family.

On October 4, the launch of the Russian satellite *Sputnik* sparked fear and concern in the United States. The Russians had beaten us in the "race to space." With the satellite passing over America at ninety-minute intervals, people wondered what the Russians could see. Could they zoom in on our top-secret facilities? Did *Sputnik* make it easier for the Reds to launch a nuclear strike? After *Sputnik II* was launched on November 3, the concern grew monumental. Politicians pointed fingers at America's National Advisory Committee for Aeronautics, or NACA. Those scientists couldn't even get the fledgling Vanguard rocket off the pad at Cape Canaveral without seeing it blow up in their faces. America's morale was low.

Orlando was also on the cusp of change. A series of devastating freezes in 1956 and '57 shook the citrus industry in Orange County. Growers began to sell their groves to speculators who wanted nothing more than the sprawling acreage they occupied. Bedroom communities were in the planning stages, and it appeared that Orlando would soon sprawl in every direction. Those who wanted the town to remain a small, agrarian Bible-belt outpost didn't like what they were seeing.

Kerouac was in high spirits. On October 14, he typed a postcard to Joyce. "I slept & slept & felt GREAT . . . play in my mind burning." He wrote the three-act play *The Beat Generation* in twenty-four hours. There were parts in it for Kerouac, Neal Cassady, Allen Ginsberg, and other friends. Using Paul Blake's typewriter, Kerouac tapped away nonstop, the lively sounds skittering out the door and into the neighborhood like mischievous alley cats.

When Joyce wrote to Jack suggesting she come down and pay a visit, he responded by distancing himself. "These next five years I will be so busy writing and publishing and producing," Kerouac told her, "I won't have time to think about l'amour." Joyce had a different take. In Florida, Jack belonged to his mother, and Joyce considered Memere "the villain." Memere often kept women away from Jack, though he would eventually marry once more. "It became apparent to me that Jack really had not separated from his mother," Johnson observed. "She had too much of a hold on him . . . any young woman who came into his life was considered the enemy."

Kerouac called his next project *Memory Babe*—the story of growing up in Lowell, Massachusetts. He thought it would be his follow-up to *On the Road*. Kerouac plunked down $1.40 for a roll of paper he said could reach from Orlando to New York City and rented a Royal Standard typewriter for just under $8 a month. Right away Kerouac liked the feel of it. "On this machine I can swing and swing and swing. I think I can go 95 words a minute on this one." Kerouac practiced on the *Diamond Sutra*, typing the 12,000-word Buddhist text on a 12-foot roll in just four hours.

Meanwhile, the editors at Viking had taken a look at the manuscripts Kerouac had brought to New York. Despite the success of *On the Road*, they flatly rejected all of them, as well as *Doctor Sax*. They wanted a straightforward book about people, no more stories about childhood. Kerouac put *Memory Babe* aside and never completed it.

In late October, Kerouac wrote a long letter to his cherished road buddy Neal Cassady. "I was wondering," Kerouac asked, "what has all this done to you, are people bugging you and chasing you in Frisco?" In his letter to Cassady, Kerouac reported that his agent had turned down a $110,000 offer from Warner Brothers to bring *On the Road* to the big screen. The studio even offered to let Kerouac play himself. But Sterling Lord held out for $150,000, and the deal never got done. There is no telling what that kind of stardom and a movie treatment of *On the Road* would have meant to Kerouac and his career.

In late November, Kerouac planned the novel that would be his follow-up to *On the Road*. Again he would approach this project like the athlete he used to be. Kerouac typed fast because, he said, life on the road is fast. He stocked up on Benzedrine for the marathon typing sessions. It would fuel his white-hot bursts of creative energy. As with *On the Road*, Kerouac planned to craft this novel on one continuous roll of teletype paper to facilitate thunderous nonstop typing. During breaks, he could shoot hoops with little Paul and knock tangerines off the tree to eat.

Kerouac kept a day-to-day journal of progress on his novel, *The Dharma Bums*. He started the novel on November 26, 1957. In a little spiral notebook Kerouac wrote in pencil, "I've got to make Dharma Bums great: Today!" In a December 2 entry he wrote, "In the midst of novel—shhh—it's coming along fine." Kerouac noted that he'd spent the night in the moonlit yard sucking three ice-cold tangerines fresh off the tree. He read *Don Quixote* and slept in a sleeping bag, his new novel already two-thirds complete. On another night in the yard, Kerouac reported seeing the *Sputnik II* satellite, "a brown star racing northward."

Kerouac finished *The Dharma Bums* at midnight on December 7, 1957. The marathon writing sessions had taken twelve days. He felt a sense of security that he had the whole story there in a 100-foot roll. But what would his editors think? "If Viking doesn't want to publish it," Kerouac wrote in his journal, "they'll be mistaken and sorry later on."

Kerouac spent much of December 8 debating the merits of his latest novel. He felt *The Dharma Bums* was "not as dramatic" as *On the Road*. But it was a better book, "technically as good in any case." He wrote that the new novel "packs explosive significance and is worth its weight in gold." Kerouac was obviously trying to convince himself that he'd written a worthy successor to *On the Road*. Then the insecurity crept in.

"Oh well, it probably stinks."

Such insecurities helped fuel Kerouac's drinking. His friend Gary Snyder (Japhy Ryder in *The Dharma Bums*) proved to be a more spiritual influence on Kerouac than Cassady. Kerouac had spent time with Snyder on a hiking trip in the Sierras in May 1956. One of their only arguments was triggered by Snyder's chiding Kerouac about his excessive intake of cheap wine. In *The Dharma Bums*, Kerouac wrote of Snyder, "This poor kid ten years younger than I am is making me look like a fool forgetting all the ideals and joys I knew before, in my recent years of drinking and disappointment, what does he care if he doesn't have any money: he doesn't need any money." Up on the mountain, Kerouac wrote that there was no need for alcohol. He promised himself that he would begin a new life.

A new life had indeed come to Kerouac, but it was not the kind he had envisioned on the mountain. With fame and attention pouring over him, he knew less peace and drank more than ever.

In December, Kerouac signed on to do a reading of his material at the legendary Village Vanguard club in New York—a gig set up by his champion from *The New York Times*, Gilbert Millstein. From his little room in the Clouser cottage, Kerouac wrote that he hoped the appearance would help put *On the Road* back on the bestseller list. He could also use the money—$500 a week. But the prospect of having to read his work before a critical New York crowd intimidated him. Back in 1952, Kerouac had often read to Neal and Carolyn Cassady while staying with them in California. "What wouldn't I have given for a chance to read my work at high money like that," Kerouac wrote plaintively in one of his little notebooks, "in the rainy roof attic on Russell St . . . O Neal and it doesn't count!"

Kerouac reiterated his nervousness to Joyce Glassman. Upon this New York trip Kerouac didn't plan to stay with her. "I dont wanta get married till I'm 69," Kerouac confessed in a letter to her. He also predicted, "This is going to be the greatest fiasco in history of American Literature, this Village Vanguard shot." If Kerouac was trying to give Joyce the brushoff, she was not so easily discouraged.

After a less than stellar opening night, an unexpected person came to the rescue. Nationally famous and host of the *Tonight* show, Steve Allen had read Kerouac's writing in a magazine and had become a fan long before Kerouac was famous. That second night, Allen slipped through the shadows and behind the piano. As Allen explained it, "I laced a few jazz licks in and around his words, in effect, 'scoring' them, rather than simply playing jazz as an unrelated background color." The music added emphasis and expression to Kerouac's reading, and the night was a success.

It still took a lot of courage and Thunderbird wine to get Kerouac up on stage. After just one week, Kerouac's Vanguard run was over. So too was 1957. At one of Kerouac's final performances, his indefatigable girlfriend Joyce slipped into a back table and watched heartbroken as the place emptied out before a drunken Kerouac could finish. Despite Kerouac's attempts to break it off with her, the two went home together. At her kitchen table, Kerouac wrote to Ginsberg, "Broke up with Joyce because I wanted to try big sexy brunettes then suddenly saw evil

of world and realized Joyce was my angel sister and came back to her."
Joyce was willing to be his girlfriend, matron, savior, secretary, and confidant. Undoubtedly, she was very much in love with Kerouac. But barely a week later, he was on his way back to the Clouser cottage in Orlando,
to Memere.

The tin-roofed Clouser house circa 1996. Jack and Gabrielle Kerouac's home during the
time when *On the Road* brought Kerouac national recognition.

A Good Neighbor

Carol Ney sitting on the steps of the Clouser house with her first edition of *On the Road*.

I've made countless visits to the little house on Clouser Avenue. One of the very first stands out in my memory:

It's mid-Saturday morning. A heavy blanket of fog envelops all sense of time. The thick mist adds a dreamlike quality to the sleepy morning as I head for Jack and Memere's former back-porch apartment. Across Lake Adair, ducks drift somewhere on the water—but could just as easily be floating in midair. Louis Armstrong's gravel yet velvet voice wafts from a jazz station I discovered on the car radio: *Give me a kiss to build a dream on.* I think of how Kerouac loved the great jazz artists. The past lingers a bit nearer in this otherworldly cocoon.

I arrive and walk around the home to the tiny back-porch apartment. I find Carol Ney and her husband, John, sitting amidst the bric-a-brac in the place they call home. Squirrels scamper in and out the back door for a handout. John sits in a straight-back chair, a blanket covering his legs. His hair is bushy and gray, and peppery whiskers dot his aged face. John's eyes look very tired, and his hearing's gone bad. He asks if I'm interested in a cigar. "Rode the rails all across the country," he tells me. "I was a hobo for years." It seems only fitting that he lives in the same place where Kerouac wrote his homage to road men like John.

Carol calls herself a retired antiques dealer, but judging from the clutter, I'd say she's had a hard time staying in retirement. Scores of old magazines line storage shelves. There's an old picture of John from bygone days and trips on the road. I take a seat in the cramped hovel. Carol begins to tell me how she used to cut out articles about Jack Kerouac when she ran across them in magazines.

"My neighbor Rose McCray knew him when he lived here," Carol recalls while lounging on her little bed and lighting a cigarette. Exhausted from the long nights of writing, Kerouac often crashed in the side yard during the day. From her home just across the street, McCray often heard Kerouac's rapid-fire typing. Intrigued by the idea of having a writer in the neighborhood, McCray wasn't shy about striking up a conversation.

"He told her he was about to get a book he'd written years ago published," Ney remembers. "And when it came out he said he'd send her a copy. Oh, and by the way, Kerouac did make good on his promise. Would you like to see it?"

See what?

Amidst all this clutter is a hidden treasure, a gift Rose McCray gave to Carol before succumbing to cancer. Sitting with her legs together on the tiny sofa bed, her gray hair pulled back in a ponytail, Carol casually reaches into a hidden place and pulls out a Ziploc bag. "You have to with all the bugs around here," she states with an air of pragmatism. When she removes what's inside and hands it to me, my heart jumps. It's a first-edition copy of *On the Road*.

The dark blue cover features a small abstract design in blue and pink. The dust jacket is frayed at the ends of the spine. The front and back covers are somewhat bent and worn. I open the book, and the 1957 price catches my eye: $3.95. On the right-hand side, another surprise, this handwritten inscription from Kerouac:

> ### To Mrs. McCray
> ### my good neighbor
> ### Jack Kerouac

Years ago, Carol saw an article that put the value of a signed first-edition hardcover of *On the Road* at $650. I told her it is worth considerably more than that today. Once, Carol said, she offered to return the gift to McCray, but she wouldn't hear of it. "No, I gave it to you," McCray had insisted, "and I want you to keep it."

It's the kind of thing you might expect a good neighbor to say.

Jack Kerouac's inscription to his neighbor Rose McCray.

Fred's Photos

Fred DeWitt outside Kerouac's back-porch apartment with an enlarged version of the photo that appeared in *Time*.

The first time I set eyes on Kerouac's notebooks in New York and the time Carol Ney produced the first-edition copy of *On the Road* she had hidden in her apartment were high points in my literary journey through Jack Kerouac's Florida years. An intriguing tip provided another heart-stopping moment in my journey.

During a freelance interview I was conducting with the late photographer, painter, and educator Bob Eginton, he asked an "oh, by-the-way" question: "Aren't you the guy doing all that research on Kerouac?" I told him I was.

"Well, then, you ought to talk to Fred DeWitt," Eginton suggested. "He photographed Kerouac in Orlando." I found out the best part later: DeWitt was not only still alive, he lived a short distance from where I worked.

For years I had searched for a visual record of Kerouac in Orlando. The only photographs I'd ever seen were a couple of stills snapped by renowned photographer Robert Frank. In April 1958, Kerouac had piled into Frank's station wagon for a road trip down to Florida. Frank had helped Kerouac and Memere move out of the Clouser back-porch apartment and up to Long Island.

Frank had taken a couple of pictures of Kerouac getting ready to leave Orlando, but as far as I knew, that was it. When I called Frank in New York to ask him about the photos, he was in no mood to be bothered. I should have taken a slower, more deferential route with the aging film-maker/photographer. But patience has never been my strong suit. Needless to say, no information was forthcoming.

In January 1958, *Time* magazine had dispatched a young photographer to shoot Kerouac for an upcoming book review. DeWitt was that young photographer.

More than four decades after that photo shoot, I found Fred DeWitt's number in the Orlando phone book and gave him a ring. He had a hard time remembering the shoot and had no idea who Jack Kerouac was. Then again, it had been a very long time. But DeWitt was a good sport and agreed to meet me over at the Clouser house. By that time, John and Carol Ney had moved on, leaving the back-porch apartment vacant.

On a sweltering August Sunday morning, DeWitt met me there, wearing black glasses and a flannel shirt much like the kind Kerouac preferred, despite the heat. Looking around, he started to clear the cobwebs from his mind. "I pulled up alongside here." DeWitt motioned to a grassy area beside the house that no one had recognized as the former driveway.

"He was waiting for me in the doorway with his left arm propped up against the doorframe," DeWitt recalled. It took a gentle shove to open the door to Kerouac's old apartment. DeWitt and I traipsed through the musty, brown-paneled sitting area. The only way to get to Kerouac's bedroom was through the bathroom. In view of Kerouac's standing as a new star of America's literary scene in early '58, it gave me pause to think of the ramshackle conditions in which he had been living.

"I remember a lone light bulb, the roll of teletype paper, and a manual typewriter," DeWitt told me while surveying Kerouac's tiny ten-by-ten bedroom. It was obvious that being there sparked DeWitt's memory. He pointed out where Kerouac's writing table had been. The men had gotten on well, talking about contemporary subjects like the Cuban revolution. Kerouac was friendly and helped DeWitt get the shots he needed. Freelance photographers will often shoot ten rolls of film even though there's space dedicated to just one picture. DeWitt wasn't like that. He had one roll dedicated to the shoot. It's right the first time—also the mantra of DeWitt's shy subject that day.

"I never even saw the images as prints," DeWitt recounted. "I just developed the roll and rushed it off to New York." In fact, the only photo from the shoot DeWitt ever saw was the one featured in *Time*'s February 24, 1958, issue. So where were the rest? "I know I don't have them," DeWitt said.

I contacted *Time*'s archivists on the off chance they might still have DeWitt's negatives in a drawer somewhere. They didn't, but to my amazement they offered to e-mail me the contact sheets of DeWitt's historic images. Would that do? Sure, it would do!

Opening the e-mail attachment a few days later was like cracking a time capsule. The first image I remember was Kerouac staring directly into the lens. Shyness seemed draped all over his face. It sent a jolt of electricity through me knowing that these frames had never been published. There's a great three-shot sequence of Kerouac sitting at his manual typewriter, examining his scroll. A series of frames shows Kerouac referring to all the little notebooks he carried while traveling. These had been the chrysalis and his books the butterflies. Another frame captures Kerouac working in the dark, illuminated only by that single light bulb. There are photos outside of Kerouac petting his cat, picking fruit, sitting alone on the back steps. There was a complete record of Kerouac retyping his *Dharma Bums* manuscript into book form. Fred DeWitt forever captured Kerouac at thirty-five, pursuing his life's passion in this hardscrabble back-porch apartment.

Compared to most of the other images of Kerouac in Florida—drunk, bloated, pathetic, or all of the above—Fred DeWitt's photos are magic. Yet even he hadn't seen them since they disappeared all those years ago. I set out to change that.

With his small, circular-framed glasses and handlebar mustache, digital photography expert Joe Brooks reminds me of Jeff Foxworthy. DeWitt came with me to watch Brooks bring these images back to life. Brooks was able to reshoot the small, contact-sheet images and download them into a computer. He could even digitally erase grease-pencil marks left by *Time*'s editors. Fred DeWitt leaned over Brooks' shoulder and watched his decades-old images become new again.

"I know you can't see it," DeWitt pointed to his long-sleeve shirt, "but watching this is standing the hair up on my arms a little bit." I had the same reaction the day I first looked at these images.

Fred DeWitt's photos establish a visual link to the most crucial time in Jack Kerouac's career, when he made the transition from nobody nomad writer from Lowell to the bard of the Beat Generation. I consider them as historic a discovery as the Clouser house itself.

While DeWitt's photographs of Kerouac were flattering, *Time's* review of *The Subterraneans* was not. The critic called Kerouac's writing "tawdry and slapdash." He proclaimed Kerouac "the latrine laureate of Hobohemia." DeWitt was terribly embarrassed by the magazine's humiliating treatment of Kerouac. "I remember going back there red-faced, with my hat in my hand," DeWitt recounted. "I told him if he wanted to take a swing at me I'd understand." But those kinds of reviews were becoming commonplace.

"It's OK, I'm used to it," Kerouac told him. "It's publicity."

By the time Kerouac moved out of this tiny apartment, his career had been transformed. He had finally made the bestseller list. He'd written for big-time magazines, received national notoriety, and ushered in a new generation of writing. In time his work would influence generations all over the world and outlast the critics and their clever lines. At the same time, Kerouac experienced the downside of fame: nasty critics, fawners, unwanted attention, and pressure to reproduce success. The boredom of hiding away in Orlando had also gotten to him. Yet barely a year later, Kerouac hoped to build a communal retreat north of Orlando for himself, Memere, and the Blakes.

Kerouac Photo Gallery

Cigar in hand, Jack Kerouac reviews the notebooks in which he sketched thoughts, poems, haiku, even entire manuscripts during his world travels. Taken in January of 1958, Fred DeWitt's photos capture Kerouac in his tiny ten-by-ten room.

It was during the time that Kerouac lived in this meager, $45-per-month back-porch apartment that he achieved literary fame and success with the publication of *On the Road*.

To escape the sometimes merciless central Florida heat and humidity in this tin-roofed, non-air-conditioned home, Kerouac often toiled long into the night.

Still, Kerouac wrote that he took "a dozen cold baths a day sweating and dying."

Kerouac said he wrote fast because life on the road was fast. Illuminated by a single light bulb, Kerouac's hands are a blur on the typewriter keys. The rapid movement suggests the great improvisational jazz artists whom Kerouac hoped to emulate with his concept of spontaneous prose.

During eleven frenetic days and nights in this room, Kerouac crafted a scroll manuscript of his *On the Road* follow-up, *The Dharma Bums*.

On breaks, he played with his cats, shot baskets, and picked citrus off the trees in his backyard.

At the time DeWitt took these photos, Kerouac was retyping his *Dharma Bums* scroll into conventional book form.

The second frame of DeWitt's three-shot sequence of Kerouac sitting at his writing desk (below, left) is the only image *Time* published in its February 24, 1958, issue. The magazine's accompanying article was a review of one of Kerouac's earlier books, *The Subterraneans*.

Time's critic called Kerouac's writing "tawdry and slapdash" and crowned him "the latrine laureate of hobohemia."

Embarrassed by the magazine's cruel treatment of Kerouac, DeWitt returned to the apartment to apologize. In an attempt to reassure the free-lance photographer, Kerouac brushed off the criticism.

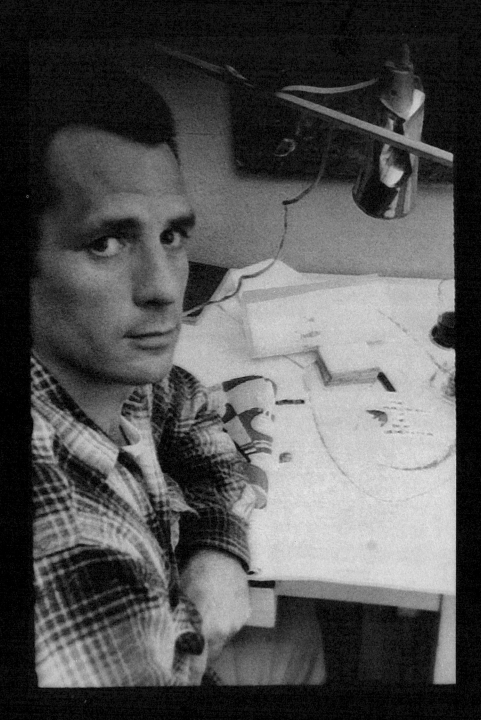

In reality, Kerouac's brother-in-law John Sampas said, "the review devastated Jack."

The Sanlando Springs Dream

1959

As for me, the basis of my life is going to be a farm
somewhere where I'll grow some of my food, and if
need be, all of it. Someday I won't do nothing but sit
under a tree while my crops are growing (after the
proper labor of course) and drink home-made wine
and write novels to edify my soul, and play with my
kids, and relax, and enjoy life, and goof off, and
thumb my nose at the coughing wretches.

Jack Kerouac

A teeming, often clogged artery runs from Daytona Beach through
the heart of central Florida. Driving on Interstate 4, Orlando-bound
commuters and fraternity boys fresh from the beach know what it's like
to hit the wall of traffic at State Road 436. On Independence Day, revel-
ers turn this patch of suburban Orlando into a veritable parking lot,
jockeying for a look at the Crane's Roost Park fireworks. It's not much
better any other time of year. You'd never guess there's an oasis just a few
miles away that evokes memories of Florida's past, the unspoiled beauty
and lack of sprawl, a place built around the perpetual bubbling of underground springs.

It was here in Sanlando Springs that Jack Kerouac once planned to
build a secluded home in the woods. About fifteen miles north of
Orlando, Sanlando Springs offered privacy and a lush tropical water
park. Around it, developers planted 10,000 azaleas. The park had a

diving platform and a waterslide. In Florida's lengthy summers, Sanlando Springs was nothing short of a cool paradise, and Kerouac had a plan to bring his whole family back together there.

For much of 1958, Kerouac felt set upon. In Northport, New York, he felt the constant prying eyes of neighbors and others fascinated by his fame. "When I write in my yard in Fla. I want no one, no EYES to be staring at me all the time, like here," Kerouac resolved. The tiny Northport newspaper feasted on gossipy details about the comings and goings in the now famous writer's household. Because Kerouac lived a scant forty miles from New York City, there were constant demands and invitations, parties and publicity, "big emergency telegrams every day," he complained. All these distractions left little time for writing. And then there was the constant worry about Memere. In January 1959 Kerouac wrote his sister Caroline, "There's alot of traveling I want to do and I can't leave Memere alone in this big lonely cold house."

In the bitter New York winter, Kerouac and his mother had forgotten the heat, isolation, and family conflict that had driven them out of Orlando barely a year before. Kerouac had convinced himself that this time it would be different. He and his mother had a plan for a communal home that would reunite them with the Blakes, who were now living in Seattle. Paul had taken a job as a rocket technician, installing weapons systems throughout the United States. Caroline wanted a permanent home base, and Kerouac hoped the Blakes would be primed to return to central Florida. "This is important," Kerouac told his sister. "And I want to go ahead with this, this year. Soon as you can."

For two families trying to converge from thousands of miles apart, the idea was complicated. Kerouac would bankroll the land and homes if his sister would oversee the construction. Their communal home would consist of an eight-room duplex. They would build two kitchens, two bathrooms, and a large patio for the whole family. Kerouac especially liked the idea of two kitchens. "It would be cute when you are making your supper in one kitchen for Paul and Lil Paul," Jack wrote to Caroline, "and Memere is making her supper in her kitchen for me and the cats. (When I'm there)."

So much of Kerouac's later existence revolved around what to do with his mother. If she wasn't content, Kerouac felt he had little hope for new travels and books. However, by March, Caroline Blake was not convinced. Kerouac and his mother continued to write letter after letter encouraging the Sanlando Springs project.

Kerouac asked his sister to come cross-country and live in Northport. At least she would be closer to Florida for some "check-up trips." Her son could attend school nearby. Two more months passed. In an attempt to speed up the plan, Kerouac put his house up for sale. With the $14,000 he expected to get for his home, the family could start construction on the duplex. Kerouac sat down and wrote his sister another letter explaining why they were so eager to get going. "I have a 3000 dollar assignment to write about Mexico for Holiday Magazine which aint hay," he informed her. To assure total privacy in Sanlando Springs, Kerouac hoped to use this money to buy one or more adjoining lots. To protect his writing retreat, he planned on building a wall around the backyard.

In June, Kerouac sold the house in Northport. By that time, Paul and Caroline had agreed to move to Florida, but because of Paul's objections, their new plan was to build separate homes side by side rather than a duplex. Memere and her daughter always shared a close bond, but the military man was not in as big a hurry to renew the family ties as his wife.

To sweeten the deal and get things moving, Kerouac offered to lend the Blakes their share of the construction money free of interest. He'd open twin checking accounts and put $7,000 in each. Caroline and Memere would live in Florida to oversee construction, and Jack would join them once the Northport transaction was final. When the Sanlando Springs homes were finished, Kerouac could concentrate on several writing assignments he'd taken on. Memere told Caroline that this might be a home where someday she would live with *her* son. "It may come in handy for you some day," Memere counseled her daughter in a letter. "I won't live forever you know."

Once Memere left for Florida, Kerouac stayed behind to tie up the loose ends on the Northport home. He felt confident that his grand plan to live in the Florida woods was about to come to fruition. It would be the final move at the end of many restless, wandering years. But from Florida came disturbing news. Memere told her son that the pressures of a cross-country move, coupled by the family entanglements, had touched off a big fight between Caroline and Paul. Deep fissures were developing in the Blakes' marriage. Caroline and her family kept trying to pull Paul back to Florida, but their plan interfered with his ambitions. Caroline and Memere left Orlando, their dream of togetherness deferred. The plans for Sanlando Springs were off.

Kerouac scrambled to find a new home in Northport for himself and his mother. Explaining to one of his editors, Kerouac blamed the weather for his decision not to move to Florida: "My Ma prefers Northport after all. New little cottage. Florida was a flooded swamp all summer."

All of the months Kerouac spent trying to arrange this move had left no time for writing. Kerouac's literary drought would go on for two more years, but one wonders what would have happened if Kerouac had succeeded in building the dream homes for his family. Would that have meant an end to the drought and another period of prodigious output? Could this have solved the internal conflicts Kerouac had when he left Memere for travels?

Probably not. Kerouac's problems were going beyond the demands of fame and his mother. By October 1959 Kerouac was roaring into an alcoholic decline. Drinking was becoming his biggest creative road-block—though Kerouac felt he needed alcohol. For a mind that had been so fertile and prolific the past decade, the next ten years were a slow suicide by attrition. There was never a home in the woods for Kerouac, only one in his mind.

In 1961 Kerouac and Memere would finally achieve the dream of living near the Blakes in Orlando. However, the death of Kerouac's Sanlando Springs plans foreshadowed turmoil ahead for Kerouac and his sister.

The Sanlando Springs property remained in the family for many years, until Paul Blake Jr. sold it in the 1970s. Today there's nothing wooded or secluded about it. Every day, those speeding along I-4 between

Longwood and Altamonte Springs drive over Jack Kerouac's dream property in the woods. A few miles away, Sanlando Springs remains a lovely but gated residential community surrounding the natural oasis that appealed to Kerouac in 1959.

In 1959 Jack Kerouac hatched and then abandoned plans to build a home in the woods near scenic Sanlando Springs.

Kingswood Manor

May 1961–December 1962

> There's a noise in the void I hear: There's a vision of
> the void; There's a complaint in the abyss—There's
> a cry in the bleak air; the realm is haunted. <u>Man
> haunts the earth.</u>
>
> ### Jack Kerouac

Audrey Redding had always assumed that meeting Hemingway's last wife, Mary, was the closest she'd ever get to literary history. Redding had met Mrs. Hemingway on a flight to Cuba in the 1950s while working as a stewardess for Delta Airlines. But the early 1960s had brought a much more substantial brush with literary genius. After Redding finished raising three boys and a girl in the suburban Orlando neighborhood of Kingswood Manor, she applied to Rollins College for her Master's. In an English literature class, she let out the little secret she'd kept for the better part of thirty years. Contemporary writers were the subject that day. Audrey casually raised her hand. "Jack Kerouac was my neighbor here in Orlando," she recounted, pronouncing his last name *Kar-oo-aahk*. She remembers the students and her professor staring with jaws hanging loosely if not entirely open.

Audrey and Dave Redding enjoy retirement in the same home they've occupied for decades. Several afternoons I've sat in their breezy front room to ask them about living across the street from the King of the Beats. Here on Alfred Drive, at the beginning of the 1960s, Kerouac had hoped to kickstart his stalled career and put his mother in a situation that would leave him free to travel. But that idyllic notion never held up, no matter how many times Kerouac tried. The Reddings remember how things went wrong for the Kerouacs and the Blakes—especially Caroline. Behind her bright bespectacled eyes, Audrey Redding still holds a fondness for Caroline and a sense of wonder about the writer who came and went like an apparition.

In 1961, Audrey liked to play tennis at the Kingswood Manor park with the rest of the young suburban housewives. They could drop their children off at the nearby playground and enjoy each other's company. During one of those sessions, Audrey's new friend, Caroline Blake, imparted what she obviously felt was good news. "My mother and brother are moving to town," Caroline said, her voice turning conspiratorial. "I guess you've probably heard of my brother—Jack Kerouac."

In November of 1960, Caroline wrote her brother with an idea. She had finally convinced Paul to relocate to Orlando, and the Blakes had bought a house in Kingswood Manor. If Kerouac and Memere decided to come down, Caroline offered to handle her brother's business affairs and keep the books for him. For years Kerouac had complained that endless letters, money matters, and curious fans kept him from getting back to travel and writing. Perhaps she could help get him organized.

Kerouac politely turned down his sister's offer. However, he began to contemplate living in Florida once more and escaping bad press and the stigma of being what is referred to today as a "deadbeat dad." While the literary success finally afforded Kerouac a comfortable living, his first wife, Joan Haverty Kerouac Aly, was struggling near poverty along with her nine-year-old girl, Kerouac's daughter, Janet. In January 1961, Joan filed a $20,000 lawsuit against Kerouac. To the press, Joan claimed Kerouac was earning somewhere around $50,000 a year from his books, though it was actually much less. Memere wrote Caroline that there was a constant stream of newspaper stories about the lawsuit.

This trouble had given Kerouac another reason to stay drunk all the time. Even Jackie Kennedy's revelation to *Time* magazine that she read Kerouac wasn't enough to ease the persecution he felt. The thought of a retreat to Orlando became more and more appealing. When a home two doors down from the Blakes went up for sale, Kerouac bought it. The ranch-style block home at 1309 Alfred Drive is the only Orlando home Jack Kerouac ever owned. In the spring of 1961, Kerouac and his mother left Northport, New York, for central Florida.

For the Kerouacs, Alfred Drive seemed to be the perfect fit. Kingswood Manor was a new development in a wooded section of northwest Orlando, not far from the Ben White horse track. For Caroline, it was a chance to have her family close by. For Memere, it meant having her son further away from the temptation of whiskey and sycophants. Kerouac described his pleasure in a May 5, 1961, letter to his agent Sterling Lord: "It was great to get out of NY and suddenly as if 'coming to America'. . . It's already hot down here but our air conditioning sends coolness from vents in every room of the house." After years of living in drab apartments and tiny homes, what Kerouac was really celebrating by moving into this fairly ordinary block home was his ascendancy to middle class.

Kerouac's home in Kingswood Manor, where he lived from May 1961 through December 1962. The only Orlando home he ever owned.

In that letter Kerouac also outlined all of the books, some written and some still in the planning stages, that would chronicle his life. Kerouac called this saga the "Duluoz Legend," or "Jack's Lifetime."

On the same day, an hour due east at Cape Canaveral, Alan Shepard blasted off to become the first American in space. America had caught up in the space race, but in the coming months, Floridians would feel the prickly heat radiating from a Communist island just 90 miles south of Key West. President Kennedy's Bay of Pigs invasion had failed to oust the young dictator of Cuba, Fidel Castro, who was spouting bravado and would soon represent a palpable threat of nuclear annihilation.

Just a few years after Jack Kerouac had become the unwitting King of the Beats, as he continued to inspire thousands of searching souls who read his books, as he and the Beats were becoming change agents and forerunners of the hippie era, Kerouac lived in an air-conditioned ranch house with his mother in the pre-Disney isolation of suburban Orlando. Her husband notwithstanding, Caroline Blake was thrilled. "It was kind of low-key hush hush," Audrey Redding remembered. "A lot of people who lived around the corner never in a million years knew he lived there." That's the way Kerouac and his mother wanted it. In letters, Kerouac often admonished friends to keep his address a secret.

Those who did know about the famous new resident rarely saw him. As during his previous stays in Florida, Kerouac often slept by day and worked by night. In the early-morning darkness, Audrey Redding often got up to nurse her new baby. A self-proclaimed "fresh-air freak," Audrey kept the windows open. Across the street she saw the red light Kerouac used in his breakfast-room writing space behind the kitchen. She could hear soft music with a flavor of the far east wafting out Kerouac's window.

It was during these early morning hours that Kerouac would write or meditate. He could hear the silky sounds of the twin pine trees out front swaying in the night air. He told family members the soft soughing of the pines reminded him of his late brother, Gerard, who had died as a child. Kerouac even had a door installed in his bedroom so he could walk into the backyard at night and listen to the wind in the piney woods. It was much to his dismay when new homes went up on Henry Balch Drive,

Kerouac's backyard to the north. "It was nice till now because of big wilderness field and woods in back," Kerouac wrote, "and now they're building 20 houses there, model homes."

Despite this disappointment, Kerouac wrote that he was content in the Florida suburbs. "I'm quiet and happy here. Play my jazz tapes, scribble, shower, read in sun, have own private door to backyard which is enclosed in 6 foot fence." Compared to the cramped back-porch apartment on Clouser Avenue, the Kingswood Manor home was a palace. The sparkling new home was appointed with cedarwood closets, formica-top bars, and an eat-in kitchen. "Livingroom is too fancy for anybody," Kerouac wrote. "Early American furniture on wall to wall rugs, the wall

Dave and Audrey Redding, close friends of Gabrielle Kerouac and Caroline Kerouac Blake during the Kingswood Manor years.

is gray, the rug is gray, and the furniture is orange and gray, cool." Kerouac spent $120 on a reclining chair he set up right next to his bookshelf, "for immediate reading." He also set up a den with a wooden rocker, rugs, and a "Japanese TV redlamp, kicks." But this middle-class appearance didn't mean Kerouac planned to completely settle in with suburbanites like the Reddings. "Across the street big boring Americans looking for togetherness. But won't get it from this old seadog."

One of Audrey Redding's most vivid memories of Kerouac came from seeing him in the early morning. "I was really amazed," Audrey remembered. "I saw him with a duffel bag marching down the street. That was really rare to see him in the daytime, especially early in the morning." But there was Kerouac, heading west towards Orange Blossom Trail, probably looking the way most of us imagine him—in his hitchhiking outfit of the day, untucked sport shirt and trousers, holding a rucksack. Memere stopped by the Reddings' place later that day, so Audrey put the question to her: "Where was Jack going?"

"Oh," Kerouac's mother said in a no-big-deal way, "he's hitchhiking to Mexico to write a book."

Kerouac left for Mexico in June 1961. He planned to write "50,000 words by candlelight." He settled into a Mexico City hotel room and wrote what would become the second half of *Desolation Angels*, which drew on his trip to Tangier in the spring of 1957. It was his first significant output in years. However, just before Kerouac left Mexico, his mood was spoiled by the theft of his packed suitcase from the hotel. When he returned to Kingswood Manor, Kerouac drank off the anger with a fifth of Johnny Walker Red a day.

Kerouac's Mexico writing provided little solace. Back home on Alfred Drive, Kerouac reviewed what he had written and felt sick. He realized how his true, sordid stories scared his family and made his sister speak in hushed, secretive tones about her own brother. His books couldn't even be bought in Orlando; they were too taboo, too controversial. Writing to his Denver buddy Ed White, Kerouac called himself a man without honor in his own house and said, "I shoulda been an architect." Kerouac's boozy summer funk made him "feel like just dropping dead." Then, in a passage that almost seems to translate as a yearning for life beyond death, Kerouac wrote, "A bright fall will come, Autumn, golden hills, me on a hill in a mackinaw, me with a bottle of wine beneath the moon, a new world, a new start."

Audrey Redding soon became Memere's confidant. At around nine on weekday mornings, after Audrey had packed her sons off to Lake Weston Elementary School, Memere would come by and hold baby Eric. Her hair in a bun, dressed in plain, old-world housewife clothes, Memere retained a kind of radiance. "She would sing French-Canadian lullabies to Eric," Audrey mused. "It was so beautiful." In this setting Memere was hardly the villain others made her out to be, just a grandmother who had raised three children of her own through difficult times.

Kerouac wrote about his mother's indelible cheerfulness despite a lifetime of hardship. "You saw her in the door, in the yard, emptying the garbage, at the stove making roasts, at the sink washing dishes, at the ironing board, all gleeful anyway." But there were episodes when Memere's thirty-nine-year-old son tested that disposition, such as the time Memere hoped to have the house carpeted. As Audrey Redding recalled, "Jack was asleep on the couch, and Memere asked the carpet man not to wake up her son. She wanted Jack to rest and keep his legs elevated to alleviate his phlebitis." In time Kerouac did wake up, and offered the stranger a drink. "And before you know it, they BOTH ended up roaring drunk!" The carpet stayed outside in a heap. Memere was not amused.

Audrey's husband, Dave, remembered how taxicabs also presented a challenge to Kerouac's temperance: "A yellow cab would show up and these strange people would unload. And boy, that did it!" Kerouac had told a small circle of friends from New York and California of his new home. When the Beat crowd descended on Kingswood Manor, just the look of them was a topic of conversation.

While the onslaught of the Beats may have brought an uneasiness to the Kerouac home, the Blakes provided an anchor for Kerouac and his mother. After the death of their brother Gerard so long ago, Kerouac and his sister had grown closer. But the two were quite different. Whereas

Kerouac was reclusive and mercurial, friends describe Caroline as outgoing and friendly. Caroline was devoted to her husband and son, and Paul Jr. credited his mother for giving him close to an idyllic childhood. Kerouac, in contrast, shunned his only daughter, left two wives, and wrote, "I dedicate myself to myself."

Caroline relished having her family so close, especially because Paul's job with the Pentagon installing weapons systems required him to travel all over the country. During one out-of-town business trip, Caroline planned a surprise. She would have an elaborate workshop added onto their home. Audrey Redding was in on it. "I'll never forget her plotting and planning. And I'll never forget how nice the workshop was. Everything was in it." The Reddings believe these were some of the best times for Caroline.

Kerouac's relationship with Paul Jr. grew steadily. Kerouac often made the two-mile hike down Edgewater Drive to walk little Paul home from Lee Junior High. A former star football player himself, Kerouac coached his nephew in track and football. During the good times, little Paul became the son Jack Kerouac never had.

Despite the fatherly qualities Kerouac exhibited with Paul Jr., he had nothing left for his own daughter. His legal battles with Joan Aly continued. In an article for *Confidential* magazine, Aly called her ex-husband "an ingrate." She was demanding "maintenance money" for herself and daughter Janet. Kerouac vehemently denied paternity. "I am going to New York to face that rat hole court," Kerouac wrote to Ed White. "Sposing the judge suddenly starts lecturing me on my evil influence on American youth or something?" Kerouac hoped a blood test or other "anthropological" means would prove he couldn't have fathered the little girl.

Meanwhile, Kerouac kept encouraging friends and business associates to visit. In late August, Kerouac wrote *Howl* publisher Lawrence Ferlinghetti, suggesting he take a detour on an upcoming trip. "On your trip to Taos and New Orleans, why not come to Orlando also and dig crazy Florida scene of spotlessly clean highways and fantastic supermarkets and Cape Canaveral and the Nova Project just 60 miles away?" Like a boy writing a friend from summer camp, Kerouac told Ferlinghetti, "My sister next door has a car, her husband has a little Sprite sportscar. Really great in October, Fla is, too, sunshine, lakes."

The year before, in the summer of 1960, Ferlinghetti had lent Kerouac his cabin in the California wilderness at Big Sur. It was at this cabin that Kerouac suffered a nervous breakdown and experienced a reawakening of his Christian beliefs. In the autumn of 1961, Kerouac sat down at the breakfast-room table of his home on Alfred Drive and made this harrowing experience the basis for his first new novel in four years. For good luck perhaps, he used what was left of the teletype paper roll on which he'd written *The Dharma Bums*.

Kerouac finished *Big Sur* on October 9, 1961. It had taken him just ten days to complete the 60,000-word manuscript. In describing the book to his agent just hours after completion, Kerouac wasn't sure how good it was. He needed to wait "for the psychological blocks to clear away" before he could stack it up against his other work. Kerouac was certain only that this was his darkest work to date. "But O so sad, this story, I vow my next book will be a Comedy and nothing else," he promised Sterling Lord.

Writing to Carolyn Cassady about his new work, Kerouac expressed some concern about the way he was continuing to use real people— including Carolyn herself—as his subject matter: "I hope you appreciate the fact that I feel, well, shamed? awful? shitty? for writing about everybody as they are." He hoped that she and others would not get mad. However, he also believed that time and art would redeem his portrayals: "But in years from now no one will see a 'mess' there, just people, just Karma."

Despite this accomplishment after years of false starts, Kerouac felt he was injuring himself by taking massive doses of Benzedrine. Between the drug and alcohol, there's little doubt he was. Yet, to celebrate his literary triumph, Kerouac went on an epic binge. In mid-October, writing to friend Philip Whalen, he described what was happening: "Got from a healthy tanned and 20 pound lighter handsome Jack to a big glooby blob of sad blufush—In no time." And it was clear the binge wasn't over: "I've just finished a fucking fifth of Martell Cognac and here I go make another drink."

Kerouac ended 1961 restless, dispirited, happy about being able to write again, but lonely. Even though his mother was now safely ensconced two houses down from her daughter, Kerouac had no great literary travels in mind. He sat and stewed in Kingswood Manor. He deliberately isolated himself from the neighbors. He'd given his address to only a small circle of friends, and most of those he invited to come down didn't. So he sat, dreamed, drank, and wrote. "What I'm actually doing is WAITING FOR SOMETHING. Somethings gotta give," Kerouac wrote in a letter to Carolyn soon after New Year's. "I'm very happy with ma and the cats but it's not enuf for a grown man, of course."

Then, in February 1962, Kerouac had to return to New York to take his paternity test. That visit was the first of only two times in her life that Janet Kerouac got to see her father. After his brief visit, Janet kept a prized memento of him, a cork from a bottle of Harvey's Bristol Cream sherry.

The blood tests proved inconclusive. Kerouac wrote to friends that he believed his first wife had conceived after she'd thrown him out in 1951, but in court papers he did admit Janet was his daughter. The judge ordered Kerouac to pay $52 a month child support until his daughter turned twenty-one. Kerouac was so relieved at the low amount that he almost invited the judge out to have a beer with him.

After Kerouac returned home, Paul Blake Jr. came over to the house to hear about his uncle's trip. As they sat in the living room talking, Kerouac pulled out a photograph of a little black-haired girl on a tricycle. "I have a daughter," Kerouac told little Paul matter-of-factly. "So that's my cousin?" Paul replied. But Kerouac cautioned the boy to keep it quiet. Memere overheard the conversation and flew into a rage. She and her son got into an angry shouting match that reverted from English to French. Like her son, Memere had refused to acknowledge Janet. Perhaps it was easier for both to deny the little girl as a blood relative than face the fact that Kerouac had abandoned her.

Several weeks after his fortieth birthday on March 12, 1962, Kerouac wrote one of his editors about his life as a literary monk in Orlando. "I am a hopeless paralyzed drunken mess, and I don't know how long I'm going to live," Kerouac reflected. "Yet I have such a good time when I'm drunk. I feel ecstasy, for people, for books, for animals, for everything. It's such a shame there's a string tied to everything huh?"

In the summer of 1962, Kerouac took to working out with weights and mowing the lawn. Again, he turned to his nephew for companionship. Now old enough to get a learner's permit, little Paul often drove Kerouac around. The "Sprite" Kerouac mentioned to Ferlinghetti was big Paul's little British sports car, and since Paul was frequently away on business trips, it wasn't hard for his son to take it for a spin. Kerouac and little Paul discovered that some of the long, vacant roads near their new subdivision made perfect drag strips. Kerouac even bought a stopwatch to time little Paul in the quarter-mile.

On one of these outings with his nephew, Kerouac may have gotten carried away by prejudice. To the east along Alfred Drive stands a wall separating Kingswood Manor from central Florida's historic black township, Eatonville. According to one Kerouac biographer, as Kerouac and his nephew passed the boundary in Paul Blake's car one night, Kerouac, fueled by cognac and whiskey, bellowed, "You ought to go burn a cross up there!" Then the two reportedly went home, erected a small plywood cross, returned to the wall, and lit it. Recalling the incident in 1997, Paul Blake Jr. stated only that he and Kerouac "almost" burned a cross together.

Incidents like the alleged cross-burning and Kerouac's occasional anti-Semitic remarks make it difficult for Kerouac scholars to deny that he had some racist attitudes. The consolation for those who knew him is that the prejudice seemed to manifest itself only after Kerouac was in alcoholic decline.

In August, the only realistic love interest from that period visited Kerouac. In 1959, while Memere was in Orlando for the aborted Sanlando Springs venture, Kerouac had met Lois Sorrells in New York. When Sorrells' mother died three years later, Kerouac proposed a visit to get her mind off things. This time someone actually accepted Kerouac's proposal. "I ben drinking and drinking and feel tremendously dejected,"

Kerouac wrote Sorrells. "You will do me as much good as two months on a mountaintop." Kerouac had finally summoned up the courage to invite a woman to his mother's home, but he would not be so bold as to share the same bed with her. In his letter he told Sorrells, "You'll be the first to use my guest room." As it turned out, the visit made Kerouac nervous, and he spent most of the time drunk. After Sorrells left, Kerouac reported to editor Bob Giroux that all the nerves and drinking made him impotent and "sad about that."

In September, five years after *On the Road*'s triumphant reception in *The New York Times*, *Big Sur* came out with a thud. *Time* magazine dismissed Kerouac's latest book as a naive look at death. Kerouac considered not publishing again. Each review stung like a personal attack.

At this point Kerouac had seven American publishers and others abroad. He couldn't keep up with all the personal correspondence. "I have to handle everything myself. Legal papers concerning taxes, deeds, shmeeds, get me so down I just get drunk and let it all pile on my desk," Kerouac complained to Stella Sampas, with whom he had kept up a correspondence since her brother Sebastian, Kerouac's good friend, had died in World War II. To his old musical collaborator, David Amram, he wrote, "I have so much mail and no time to buy envelopes ugh, fame is a drag to anybody who wants new work done."

Kerouac's drinking had now increased to the point where he suffered severe blackouts. He was making excuses to hide his alcoholism. When a family friend called, Kerouac claimed to be sick, but he failed to explain the cause—delirium tremens brought on by excessive drinking. In those final few months on Alfred Drive, Dave Redding said that Kerouac "looked beat. The phlebitis and the alcohol and all the other stuff. He was a worn-down person."

Kerouac's internal disintegration seemed to be mirrored in the family disintegration he saw around him. By late 1962, the only two families Kerouac felt close to were imploding. From California, Kerouac received word that Neal and Carolyn Cassady were on the verge of divorce. Caroline's marriage to Paul Blake was also in trouble, due in part to tension with Kerouac and his mother. Paul Blake Jr. recalled his father's resentment when Kerouac, Caroline, and Memere spoke French. That meant Paul Sr. was excluded from the conversation. "Dad didn't want any bilingual in the house," his son said. Blake was spending more and more time out of town and drifting further from his wife and son.

Memere was depressed because the two families were barely speaking. Despite the bitterness, Kerouac loaned the Blakes money to complete an addition to their house, but he resented bankrolling what he saw as their "needless luxuries." On one occasion Kerouac gave Paul Sr. a $7 bottle of scotch and reported that he didn't get so much as a "thank you." In a journal passage that foreshadowed the legal battles long after his death, Kerouac wished for God to make him a millionaire so he could have the satisfaction of leaving nothing to the Blakes after he died.

The time was near for another move, Memere agreed. In November, while waiting for a $1,350 article fee from *The Saturday Evening Post*, Kerouac picked out a house back in Northport, New York. Money problems had forever destroyed Kerouac and Memere's fantasy of living with the Blakes as a happy, extended family. Years later, remembering what the families had tried to accomplish, Kerouac wrote, "Togetherness America. Nobody's gonna pull that shit on me."

One day in late December 1962, the Reddings' doorbell rang. Standing there in the doorway was Jack Kerouac—the man who'd spent much of his time as a pre-dawn, after-dusk mystery to the neighbors. He couldn't leave without saying something to Audrey. "I just wanted to come over and thank you for being such a good friend to my mother," Kerouac told her.

A few days before Christmas, Kerouac, Memere, and their three cats boarded a train for New York. Over the past six years, they had lived in Orlando three times. The stay on Alfred Drive was the last and longest, but the relationship between the Kerouacs and the Blakes was now irretrievably broken.

Jack and the Boys of Summer

In 1961, no one would have thought Paul Gleason and Mickey McDermott were on their way to the fame and fortune they both found later. Few will ever remember them for their achievements in baseball. But if there were a drinking and carousing hall of fame, the two would be right there in Stuporstown. In Jack Kerouac, Gleason and McDermott found a kindred spirit. All three men were at low points in their careers when they met at Orlando's baseball stadium.

As a diversion from suburban, humdrum Orlando isolation, Kerouac was drawn to Tinker Field. Dwarfed by the Citrus Bowl just west of downtown Orlando, Tinker Field has hosted its share of baseball greats, including Babe Ruth, Stan Musial, and Jackie Robinson.

"Kerouac was always there sitting in the stands," Gleason recounted. "Hotter than hell and he'd have a raincoat on." A self-described baseball bum at the time, Gleason had a trick for catching on with teams. After one released him, Gleason would sign on under a false name. "Oh, I was Paul Benson in the Carolina League . . . I played under the names Billy Gleason, Paul Gleason." That would last awhile until the team found out who he really was, or until Gleason's talent ran out and he was let go. In Orlando, Gleason played third base. In class D ball, the games were so small and intimate that if a player wanted a drink or a hot dog, he straddled the chain-link fence and stood in line with the fans.

Mickey McDermott had fulfilled his destiny as one of baseball's greatest underachieving pitchers. By the time he ended up as the Orlando team's pitching coach, McDermott's 100-mph fastball was a distant memory, and he already had his bookend sixty-nine career wins and losses. His scotch consumption was legendary. After long benders, cDermott would sleep them off on the screen porch of the dump he was renting in Orlando. "I'd have to turn the hose on him full bore through the screen to wake him up," Gleason recalled.

Kerouac had met McDermott years before at a club called Steuben's in Boston. The two renewed their friendship in Orlando. Gleason was just twenty-one at the time he met Kerouac, and in some ways he was very different from Kerouac. "I was the antithesis of a literate person," Gleason said. Kerouac's stories of life with Neal Cassady in *On the Road* didn't impress Gleason at all.

However, Kerouac and Gleason shared several common bonds. Both were standout college football players, Kerouac at Columbia University and Gleason at Florida State University. After a few drinks, the men reverted to their college days. "We used to get down in the dirt and go one on one," Gleason said. "Sometimes we didn't stop until someone drew blood." They also shared a deep admiration for the baseball player Kerouac always referred to reverently as "Number 9"—Ted Williams.

Kerouac used to love to watch Ted Williams play at Fenway Park, and since Gleason had recently played in the Red Sox organization with Williams, Kerouac loved hearing Gleason's stories about him. Given Kerouac's growing hatred of literary critics at that time, he especially enjoyed hearing Gleason tell about how Williams tortured his own critics, the sports writers.

Williams often retaliated with silence. Since writers could not get quotes directly from Williams, they sometimes hit up Gleason for details of his conversations with the Red Sox great. "What did Teddy say?" they implored the young ballplayer. "Oh nothin' much," Gleason told them. One day, some writers tried creeping down the bench to hear what Williams was telling Gleason.

As Gleason told this story, his voice exploded just as Williams' did. "I SEE YOU SONS OF BITCHES! YOU C—SUCKERS, YOU MOTHER F—KERS! GET THE HELL OUT OF HERE! I AIN'T TALKIN' TO YOU." Gleason remembered, "They scattered down through the tunnel like rats out of a burning house, all three of 'em."

Gleason believed that this kind of bravado, spontaneity, and outspokenness is what drew Kerouac to Williams. "He let things flow," Gleason said of Williams. "And that was what Kerouac looked for in everything in life—people who didn't revise their behavior, didn't conform." Kerouac told Gleason of hitchhiking from Lowell to Boston in 1939 to watch Williams play. "The thing I loved about Williams was his glee," Kerouac commented. "He had great glee."

One particular aspect of Kerouac that stayed with Paul Gleason so many years after the men shared an association was Kerouac's emotional sensitivity. As Kerouac shared a story of his late brother, Gerard, he broke down. "It was the first time I ever saw a grown man cry," Gleason said, with still a hint of wonder in his voice. But he did not see Kerouac as being sad or depressed a lot—quite the opposite. "If there's a word I can use to describe Kerouac during that time," Gleason reflected, "it would be *giddy*." Whether they were going to the movies together, hitting the bars, or hanging out at the ball field, Kerouac enjoyed jokes and laughter.

With two new baseball buddies to follow, Kerouac often came to Tinker Field early. Gleason remembers an exchange he and Kerouac had when the writer stood in the front row just behind the chain-link fence. Gleason threw baseballs at his feet and ordered playfully, "Dance, Kerouac; you're killing the grass."

In the still-segregated south of the early 1960s, Kerouac sat with black fans in the bleachers down the left field line to pick up on the way they talked. He always carried a book in his back pocket and a pen or pencil in the front with which to take notes or draw.

Gleason still has a pencil drawing of Kerouac's that used to hang in his locker at Tinker Field. There's a crudely drawn crucifix. Next to it are a couple of ghostly-looking characters with what appear to be halos above their heads. At the bottom he signed it—*Jack Kerouac*. This was something Kerouac often did for friends to authenticate their friendship with him, as if he knew his doodles and signature would be worth something someday.

Gleason knew he was going nowhere in baseball. "I was rootless," Gleason reflected, "and I didn't have an education." For Gleason, change came in a darkened Orlando movie theatre with Kerouac and Mickey McDermott. The ballplayers picked up Kerouac at his home on Alfred Drive, intent on seeing a matinee showing of *Splendor in the Grass*. Kerouac's old running buddy from his New York days, David Amram, had done the score for the film. Warren Beatty played a young football player. The cocky young Gleason said, "Ah hell, I could do that. Maybe that'll be my next gig." Soon Gleason's passion for acting caught fire, and he put down his glove for good. Gleason called that day in the Orlando movie theater with Kerouac and McDermott "a watershed moment in my life."

Gleason joined the Actors Studio in New York City. His teacher was Elia Kazan, director of *Splendor in the Grass*. Gleason went on to play MacMurphy in an off-broadway adaptation of Ken Kesey's *One Flew Over the Cuckoo's Nest*. In the 1970s, he caught on as Dr. David Thornton in the ABC daytime drama *All My Children*. In the 1980s and beyond, Gleason had numerous high-profile roles in films such as *The Breakfast Club*, *Trading Places*, *The Great Santini*, and *Die Hard*.

Gleason was shocked and amazed when I told him there had been talk of Kerouac playing himself opposite Marlon Brando in a film adaptation of *On the Road*. "Kerouac would have been a great actor," Gleason extolled, "because he always had emotions at his fingertips, and he was always very spontaneous." As Gleason's success as an actor grew, he drew more and more on his time with Kerouac for artistic inspiration. He also got to know some of Kerouac's Beat writer friends such as John Clellon Holmes. At a Beat literature conference in Colorado in the early 1980s, Gleason ended up having a conversation with Jan Kerouac in a hot tub. "I told her she had the same hands as her father," Gleason reflected.

Gleason's baseball buddy from the Orlando days, Mickey McDermott, hit it big in a much different way. In 1991, after years of nearly killing himself drinking and carousing, the washed-up pitcher won $7 million in the Arizona state lottery. He got sober, cleaned up his life, and wrote a book about it. Imagine the irony.

The pencil image Kerouac drew for baseball buddy Paul Gleason, which hung in Gleason's locker at Tinker Field. Courtesy of Paul Gleason.

Kenny's Discovery

I turn past the big white letters that spell out Kingswood Manor. It's a windows-down, clear, evocative evening. Like a magic nightlight, the big, round moon emerges from a cloudless blue blanket. In the years since Kerouac lived here, Orlando has grown up and around this old subdivision. I'm inching my way down Kingswood Drive, but it might as well be Memory Lane. Blot out the cars and satellite dishes and it's 1962 again.

A little wisp of a dog wearily checks out the stranger rousing him from the middle of the street. Plastic ducks and ducklings peer over a little white picket fence. Porch lights illuminate stuccoed arches of the block home entryways. Their roofs, either flat or pitched at a slight angle, hold solar heating panels for warm pools year-round. The carports, some open and bright, have chairs and couches that invite the company of neighbors, suggesting a time before closed-in garages and the need to lock up every possession for fear of crime and the unknown. The lighted tennis courts of Kingswood Manor Park allow two friends a late game.

I pull a U-turn at Lake Weston Elementary, a school attended by neighborhood kids for decades, and turn down Alfred Drive to talk to a man I'll bet Kerouac would have been glad to call a friend.

Kenny Sears read *On the Road* for the first time in 1973, back when Sears says he was very much the "teen-aged hippie." At a party one night, a friend gave him the book. Sears couldn't put it down and ended up reading it all in one night. Sears' neighbors across the street, Audrey and Dave Redding, had always been like another set of parents to him. Since they had a whole wall full of books, Sears asked if they might have any others by "this guy Kerouac." No, but they did have a little secret they thought they'd share with him.

Since 1966, Ken Sears has lived at 1309 Alfred Drive, the only Orlando home Kerouac ever owned. When I first talked to Ken on the phone, he said, "This was one fantastic thing, but then one one would believe me." He explained how he had made a search through the abstract title to his home and found proof. In a document dated May 29, 1961, Gabrielle Kerouac's signature appeared at the bottom of a $16,000 mortgage. Among the names of those living there at the time, Jack Kerouac. It was all the evidence Sears needed.

I show up at the house on Alfred Drive a little early and wait a few minutes until Kenny Sears comes home from work. As I enter the house, I notice that the family room sports that original speckled terrazzo tile, still no carpeting. On the wall is a pink rotary phone, also original with the house. An unusual brick wall painted white separates the family room from what used to be Kerouac's writing space. Immediately, I can picture him blazing away on his novel *Big Sur.*

Sears and I have planned to spend the evening talking about Kerouac. He offers me a beer and I accept. It seems only fitting, considering our subject for the night.

Sears is in his early forties, with black hair and a mustache that tends to hide his sad but friendly smile. He ends many of his sentences with *buddy,* and he likes to talk about the experience of living in "Jack's house." Sears says that sometimes someone drives slowly down the street and does a double-take in front of his home. "Hippies would show up," Sears recalls. "Did Jack Kerouac live there? And I'd say, 'yeah, you wanna see the house?'"

Once a cameraman was hired to shoot some footage of the home for a film project. He and Sears savored a few beers, and before long, the cameraman was sprawled out on the family room couch, just like the Kerouacs' carpet installer all those years ago. Sears chuckles about that night. "He finally sobered up enough to put his equipment back in his Volkswagen van and go home."

Before it gets too dark, we walk outside in the backyard. The home still has the old basket-weave type fence that Kerouac had installed to protect

Ken Sears standing next to the door Kerouac had cut out of the bedroom wall.

his privacy. I snap a couple of pictures of Sears standing by the door Kerouac cut out of the bedroom. There's no sign of the woods out back that Kerouac loved.

I sense loneliness in Ken Sears, but also a great deal of openness and honesty. He shares with me how his mother died unexpectedly and he almost didn't have the will to go on. Years later, he was also forced to come to terms with his brother's illness and death. I sense a parallel between Sears and what an interviewer once wrote about Kerouac: "Like a little boy, an eternal innocent, he had no defenses." Though Sears doesn't pretend to be an expert on Kerouac or his writing, he feels he can say, "I know this guy was something special in his life."

People have gone so far as to suggest Sears make a bed and breakfast out of the house or charge money for tours. "I'm always trying to think of a way to make some more money," Sears concedes. "I wouldn't make it off him, though—nah." Time slips past quickly. Sears offers me a friendly embrace and says goodbye.

So much happened to Kerouac and his family on this seemingly unremarkable street, in this typical suburban Orlando neighborhood, where Kerouac spent two summers of discontent and his sister's life started to fall apart. As my car moves slowly away from Ken Sears' house, and then the Blakes' old house two doors down, it is all on my mind.

Kerouac spent parts of five years in Orlando. The College Park years marked his ascendancy to literary fame, promise, and family respectability. Kerouac's time on Alfred Drive drove him further into bitterness over critics, money problems, paternity issues, family conflict, literary failure, the lack of a love interest, and a generally rudderless life built around his mother's happiness at the expense of his own.

Beneath a radiant full moon, I make my way out of Kingswood Manor, through the maze of roads and time.

ST. PETERSBURG

1964–1969

Yacht Basin and Harbor, St. Petersburg, Florida, "The Sunshine City"

Locked in Grief
1964

The last time I saw her I gave her hell.

Jack Kerouac

After Kerouac moved from Kingswood Manor back to Northport, New York, the familiar problems crept back into his life. Curious teen-aged hoodlums forced him to stand guard in his own house with a homemade tomahawk, and his paranoia grew. Many people wanted to visit the Kerouacs. "Mind you, when they come they stay three to four days and that's too much for me," Memere complained to her daughter. But Memere also noted, "Jack is weeding out friends he don't want around here so we can have peace."

For Kerouac, the peace that Memere wanted often led to the same isolation and boredom he had suffered in Orlando. This time he didn't even have young Paul or his baseball buddies to pal around with. Boredom led to more drinking. Kerouac's latest releases, including *Visions of Gerard,* which was published in 1963, were not selling well. The frequent moves and cash down payments had left Kerouac strapped financially, and money from foreign royalties was all that kept him afloat. He felt the strain of the largest mortgage he had ever had to pay, along with monthly child support.

Time and distance did not mend the wounded relationship between the Blakes and the Kerouacs, though they managed to exchange some cordial letters. Kerouac agreed to loan his sister $3,000, which she promised to pay back in thirty installments of $100. Kerouac's own financial problems meant he needed the Blakes to pay back the loan on time. Soon he was so concerned that he arranged for a face-to-face meeting with his sister and brother-in-law. In October 1963, Kerouac boarded a plane for Orlando to collect. Flying always made Kerouac jumpy— another reason to imbibe. By the time he arrived in Orlando, Kerouac was drunk. At the Blakes' home, he was so belligerent that Caroline called the police. "Got escorted to the airport by the sheriff at my sister's instigation," Kerouac recounted. "Don't remember the return flight at ALL." By all accounts, this was Kerouac's last trip to Orlando and the last time he saw his sister alive.

In 1964, with no end in sight to the financial problems, Memere insisted on a move back to sunnier, cheaper Florida. Kerouac agreed, but only on the condition that they put some space between themselves and the Blakes. They settled on St. Petersburg, a sleepy gulfside city about an hour-and-a-half's drive from Orlando.

Jack Kerouac's main confidant during this time was his agent, Sterling Lord. Upon Kerouac and Memere's move to 5155 Tenth Avenue in St. Petersburg in early September, Lord was the first person Kerouac wrote. "I lost some on my Northport house but we just had to get out of there and it was worth it," Kerouac told Lord. "This is a stimulating city."

Unlike the isolated Kingswood Manor, Kerouac's new neighborhood was close to everything. He could walk to the store or library, and he soon developed a group of younger drinking buddies. He shot pool and went to minor league baseball games at Al Lang Stadium.

One of the first people Kerouac and his mother met upon their arrival in St. Petersburg was Nell Burrow, who lived in the big corner ranch house next door. Nell's husband, Tex, had built Kerouac's home on Tenth Avenue. The Burrows had a daughter, Cheryl. It was Nell who helped her new neighbors get settled.

"They didn't have anything with them, so I took some cooking ware over—and a coffee pot," Nell remembered. "It was like I'd known 'em all my life." Nell had taken a shine to Memere right away, and even at this stage in Kerouac's life, she found him one of the most handsome men she had ever met, with the blackest hair she'd ever seen. Kerouac and his mother appreciated the Burrows' kindness while they waited for their own furniture to be delivered. They slept on borrowed cots for the first ten days in their new home.

Nell Burrow witnessed Kerouac's daily routine. Since Kerouac still didn't drive, on jaunts to the nearby Publix grocery store he often pulled a little laundry cart behind him. Many times Nell and Cheryl spotted him talking to the towering pine tree in his front yard, no doubt feeling closer to his sainted brother. Other times, Kerouac sat in the shade jotting down his thoughts. "He'd always carry a little notebook with him," Nell Burrow remembered.

Financially, 1964 was another rough year for Kerouac. His earlier books were going out of print and *Big Sur* was not selling, so he supplemented his income by writing magazine articles for the likes of *Playboy* and *Holiday*. By September, Kerouac's income for the year so far was $2,500. But at least St. Pete offered a lower cost of living. The rent was low, and there was no phone bill or car payment. When he needed to get out of the house, Kerouac strolled down to the Tic Toc lounge for a game of pool.

Although relations with his sister were strained, Kerouac tried to reach Caroline by telephone. He and Memere knew there was trouble in her marriage. Paul Sr. had all but abandoned his family. To help Caroline make ends meet, the Kerouacs had continued to loan her money, and Jack estimated she now owed him $5,000.

A strange transformation had taken place in the relationship between brother and sister. When Jack was living in Orlando, his sister was the caretaker. More than once Caroline had gotten the call from beachside police departments to come and retrieve her brother from the gutter. But after her marriage began to disintegrate, Caroline became the needy one, and Jack became the financial provider. In the end, when Caroline's life fell apart and she needed her brother and mother around more than ever, money issues had created a barrier between them.

Unable to reach Caroline by phone, Kerouac called an old friend in Kingswood Manor, Audrey Redding.

"One day the phone rang and it was Jack," Audrey Redding remembered. "He was very upset. He said he couldn't find his sister."

By that time, the Reddings were painfully aware that Caroline's good times in suburban Orlando were over. She had tried to hold onto her house and at least the image that all was well with her family. However, despite loans from her brother, Caroline had tried to sell furniture to the neighbors. Finally, when Paul left her to move in with another woman, Caroline sold the house on Alfred Drive.

Caroline and Paul Jr. were now living at the 14th Fairway Apartments along Dubsdread Golf Course in College Park. Caroline kept the books and helped manage the property. The two-story, eight-unit block walkup stood a short distance from Paul's school, Edgewater High.

Caroline was back in College Park but under much different circumstances. It had to have been a difficult step down from the good life in Kingswood Manor. Caroline mowed lawns and did whatever she could to make ends meet. In addition to her financial difficulties, the breakup of her family was a tough psychological blow for her. She was trying alone to raise a teen-aged son, who sometimes didn't come home for days and other times flooded the apartment with his friends. There was also a stigma attached to divorce. As one of Paul Jr.'s old school chums told me, "No one got divorced in those days." For Caroline, a failed second marriage had to be a tremendous source of shame and psychological strain. With all the stress, her weight dipped to 90 pounds.

On Saturday afternoon, September 19, 1964, Caroline was on the phone with Paul Blake Sr., who was now living with his mistress in Washington, D.C. During that phone call, Caroline's husband of two decades told her their marriage was over. Distraught, Caroline replied, "if that's the way you want it." And with that, she apparently suffered a severe heart attack and died. Her son found his mother passed away on the couch when he came home from getting sodas. A cup of tea was still resting on the sofa arm.

Jack Kerouac returned from a night of playing pool to find his disconsolate mother in the doorway. Caroline was dead, she told him. Although those initial days after Caroline's death, knowing he was the only surviving sibling, must have been terribly difficult for Kerouac, he wrote nothing in his journal to mark his sister's death.

On Monday, September 21, a few friends gathered at the Garden Chapel Funeral Home to say goodbye to Caroline. The next day they met again at Greenwood Cemetery. Memere made the trip to Orlando without her son. Too grief-stricken to go, Kerouac locked himself in the bathroom of his St. Petersburg home.

Paul Blake Sr. made a scene at the wake, weeping openly and promising Memere that somehow he'd make it up to his dead wife. Gabrielle reassured him in her French-Canadian accent, "Yes, Paul. I know, Paul." The Reddings were seething at what they perceived was "blatant pretense." Dave Redding remembered the anger he felt then towards Paul Blake Sr. "Oh sure, now you want to make it up to her. Why didn't you treat her better the last two years of her life, you son of a bitch?" According to Audrey, "Dave would have gladly killed him right there on the spot." But Dave Redding kept his anger in check.

The Reddings still did not know of the rift between Caroline and her mother and Jack. Looking back on Caroline's last days, Audrey reflected, "She must have felt completely abandoned and hopeless. More than ever I believe that she died of a broken heart."

Kerouac shared this opinion. Four weeks after his sister's death, he wrote a morose letter to his old friend John Clellon Holmes. "Her husband left her and broke her heart, period," Kerouac stated. "Nin had a loyal heart, which that cracker couldn't begin to understand." But Kerouac also entertained the possibility that the day-to-day chaos of his sister's life and the responsibility of single motherhood contributed to her death.

Kerouac's sadness was exacerbated by a lingering sense of guilt. The money he had loaned his sister's family had driven a wedge between himself and the Blakes. The last time Kerouac had seen his sister, in 1963, he was so drunk and belligerent that she was forced to call the cops. It was all about money. When Caroline was frail and alone, trying to raise her son and put her life back together, she had no family around to help. It all weighed heavily on Kerouac. "The last time I saw her I gave her hell," he lamented.

With both his brother and his sister gone, Kerouac was forced to take a deeper look at his own mortality. "Get older and you get more mystified. Youth has a way of sloughing off death and graves," Kerouac reflected in his letter to Holmes. "When in real life there's a red neoned funeral parlor on the end of your street, the gloom hits you." Late at night, Kerouac would sit out on the front porch. Only now the pine tree's soft soughing reminded him of two lost siblings.

Kerouac and his mother both turned to alcohol to deaden the pain. Kerouac started bingeing on scotch with beer chasers. On Thanksgiving night of 1964, a reckless bender cost him. "The cops saw me piss in the street," Kerouac reported. "First time in jail."

For Nin

A steamy Sunday afternoon isn't the best time to go walking around an old Florida cemetery, but I couldn't resist. Since 1880, eighty thousand Orlandoans and their stories have been buried here. I was after only one. It was Memorial Day, and I was taking a little time-travel in honor of Caroline Kerouac Blake. I wondered what kind of remembrance Kerouac and Memere had fashioned for her. Since Caroline had been a member of the Women's Air Corps in World War II, I brought along a little American flag to decorate her grave.

Greenwood Cemetery is Orlando's oldest public cemetery. In its location just south of the teeming East-West Expressway, it offers a microcosm of the city, past and present. From the northwest corner, headstones face an ever-growing skyline. The tall, gleaming Orange County Courthouse and a cluster of new buildings surrounding City Hall stand in tribute to central Florida's run of economic prosperity. As tourism goes, so goes Orlando. It's a giant metropolis compared to the city that Caroline and Paul Blake first called home in 1956.

Greenwood also has an adjoining urban wetland where one might spy a blue heron posing like a statue or a graceful white egret taking flight. All are still plentiful despite the continual human encroachment. The surrounding neighborhood with its older bungalows and shady, tree-lined streets has benefited from urban renewal. Young families in brightly painted older homes go about their busy lives near a cemetery that's every bit the size of a college campus.

For more than a century, Orlandoans have buried their war dead here. I passed row after row of aligned stones dedicated to the young soldiers who died in Korea. Many of Orlando's early settlers and prominent citizens are also buried here, including baseball great Joe Tinker. Then there are those who didn't have a chance to make their mark: a thirteen-year-old boy whose headstone carries a poem about deer hunting; the blond- haired youth who died at age twenty in the year that *On the Road* came out. Staring back at me in black T-shirt and cut-off sleeves from the picture on his headstone, he looked like the kind of free spirit who would have liked *On the Road.*

Caroline Blake's cremated remains were buried here on September 22, 1964. The cemetery office was closed, so I enjoyed the relaxed pace of trying to find her grave on my own. My thoughts turned to Memere. She had such optimism over the years that her family might overcome their difficulties to live together in a happy Florida home. What misery she must have suffered that day here at Greenwood Cemetery! She had come to bury her only daughter, dead at forty-five, her only surviving son too upset to attend. Though the Kerouacs were Catholic, a Baptist preacher from College Park had prayed over Caroline's remains.

The small American flag marks Caroline Kerouac Blake's grave at Greenwood Cemetery in Orlando.

Still walking and searching, I remembered some of Jack's fond memories of himself and his sister. Their parents always used the French word *Ti*, for *little*, when referring to their children. There was the time when Ti Nin was ten and Ti Jack just eight. The siblings were enamored by the brawny build of a family friend. "Show us your muscles," the children beseeched. When the friend obliged, "Nin hung from one bicep," Kerouac remembered, "and I hung from the other, whee." In adulthood Caroline's personality might have been the polar opposite of her brother's, but their bond endured through the years.

A worker noticed my wandering and helped me with a map. I followed the trail that he outlined in red. In section four, 80 feet or so behind the double marker of the Martinsons, just to the left of Edna Bourque's grave, under the soothing shade of a maple tree, was—an empty patch of grass. *This can't be it*, I told myself. There was nothing there.

The cemetery worker confirmed it—no sign or stone to mark the passing of Caroline Kerouac Blake. I was shocked. This was, after all, the woman immortalized in many of Kerouac's books and in books about him. She's forever part of the life story he liked to call the "Legend of Duluoz." My heart sank as I stood looking at Caroline's final resting place. I placed the little United States flag on the empty patch of ground.

After my visit to the gravesite, in a phone call to Paul Blake Jr., I asked what had happened. "My father always planned to put up a stone in her memory," Paul told me. Maybe that was one of the promises Paul Sr. made to Memere. He had eight years to do it and never did. After Caroline's death, he moved to southern California and eventually remarried. He pressured his son to move to California, too, though Paul Jr. begged his father to let him stay in Orlando and finish his last two years of school at Edgewater High. His grandmother and Uncle Jack were not living close enough to Orlando to be considered in the scenario. Paul Sr. refused, telling his son he'd have the police escort him to the airport if necessary. Paul Jr. relented, despite the fact that he blamed his father for his mother's death and the breakup of their family.

Paul Jr. told me his father never got over Caroline's death. Paul Blake Sr. died in a car crash in 1972. And Paul had more unexpected news: his father's cremated remains were buried along with Caroline's in that unmarked patch of ground. Nin is thrust together forever in anonymity with the man who broke her heart. There are no words for them or between them. So here I'll make my own:

Caroline Kerouac Blake
October 25, 1918
September 19, 1964
Mother, Daughter, Sister, Wife
Veteran
Je Me Souviens, Ti Nin

Running with the Lion
1965

As I grew older I became a drunk. Why?
Because I like ecstasy of the mind. I'm a wretch.
But I love love.

Jack Kerouac,
Satori in Paris

I made my way down the long, shotgun-barrel-straight bridge that spans Tampa Bay, connecting Tampa and St. Petersburg. I was heading to a mid-town St. Pete Denny's restaurant to meet up with one of Kerouac's buddies from the 1960s. Although the rest of central Florida is hardly known for its dramatic topography, I'm still taken aback by how flat the region is. St. Petersburg itself is a quiet town, where the days seem to move to drowsy, laid-back rhythms.

Several people had told me that Ron Lowe had a unique take on Kerouac's later life. Lowe had assumed a cult-figure status of his own in his hometown. In 1962, Lowe's band became the first to break the color barrier on the beaches, having interracial members and playing to integrated audiences. At that time they were hired as the house band at the Peppermint Lounge on Madeira Beach. Like Kerouac's, Ron Lowe's musical tastes were color-blind. A local black deejay said the band was like dominoes. The idea stuck.

"White in spots," Lowe liked to say, "but mostly black."

At the restaurant where we agreed to meet that day, the first thing that struck me about Ron Lowe was his hulking frame, and soon after, the size of his intellect. We exchanged greetings and took a booth. In Ron Lowe's hand was an old brown briefcase containing his tangible links to Kerouac. In his head were the memories of being a companion, protector, devil's advocate, buddy, confidant, but never a "yes man" of the fading Beat icon.

At first, Lowe told me, he wasn't much impressed with the man to whom he'd been introduced that afternoon in 1965 during a Twilight Lounge gig for his band, Ronnie Lowe and the Dominoes. On a break, an old schoolmate introduced him to a guy claiming to be Jack Kerouac. Lowe wasn't about to fall for it. The disheveled man in a T-shirt and baggy pants bore no resemblance to a literary legend, whatever one is supposed to look like. This man was just telling tales and taking up space.

"Two sheets to the wind," the stranger didn't seem all that thrilled to make Ron Lowe's acquaintance either. "But the guy was no barstool fool. The way he spoke was pure poetry," Lowe recounted. So the big burly bass player made his way back towards the ragged man and tried to pretend he wasn't listening to him. The two once again exchanged words.

Jack Kerouac's first home in St. Petersburg.

Soon after, the stranger demanded that Lowe give him a ride home. The request was just outrageous enough for Lowe to agree.

As the two cruised through St. Petersburg in Ron Lowe's car towards an address the stranger gave him, Lowe kept wondering, "Could it be? The now legendary King of the Beat Generation hanging out in a St. Pete honky-tonk?" They pulled up to the little one-story ranch house near the corner on Tenth Avenue. The passenger offered Lowe a couple of dollars for gas money. When Ron refused to accept it, the stranger said, "C'mon in, we'll listen to some good music."

Inside the house, the books and writerly goods confirmed for Lowe that this man was indeed Jack Kerouac. Kerouac dashed between a pair of old Webcor reel-to-reel tape decks, Mozart playing on one side of the room, Zoot Sims on the other. That first meeting sparked a friendship that would last until the day Kerouac died.

Lowe's polite, southern *yes-ma'am, no-ma'am* gentility appealed to Memere. Normally protective of her son, Memere told Lowe, "I don't mind if Jackie goes out with you because you'll take care of him." It was as if she was referring to them both as twelve-year-old boys.

Ron Lowe was twenty years younger than Kerouac, and he looked like a defensive tackle. Lowe made for an intimidating presence when Kerouac's alcohol-induced bombast threatened to ignite barroom fisticuffs. In early March of 1965, Kerouac was indeed severely beaten in a bar fight and suffered two broken ribs.

The younger Lowe held in high esteem the man he called "the American mystic writer-poet, mysterious lion of the international literary underground." But Lowe was no starry-eyed sycophant, ready to let Kerouac get away with anything, nor did Kerouac care for those who wanted to shower him with empty praise and bask in what was left of his fame.

The manager of the Twilight Lounge had a little apartment up on the roof of the place. Sometimes Lowe managed to spirit a groupie up to his fantasy bachelor pad. Other nights, Kerouac joined him for hours of conversation. On one such night, Kerouac bellowed to the stars, "Hemingway and Melville are spinning in their graves tonight, calling out to each other, 'who is this new guy?'" Ron Lowe could tell that Kerouac knew celebrity had passed him by but literary immortality would not.

Lowe's story reminded me of a passage from *On the Road* in which Sal Paradise spends a night partying in Central City, a mountain town west

Ron Lowe, band leader and Kerouac's buddy during the St. Petersburg years, 1964–69.

of Denver: "We fumed and screamed in our mountain nook, mad drunken Americans in the mighty land. We were on the roof of America, and all we could do was yell."

In a newspaper article about Kerouac, Ron Lowe wrote, "He instigated many nights of intense talk and debate, and if I finally dropped him off at three in the morning there was an even chance he'd be knocking at my door in the dawn's earliest light, waving off the cabby with a cheery, *You can go now. My friend is at home.*"

When the Dominoes finished their Twilight Lounge sessions, it was their traditional democratic process to vote on a place to share the post-jam repose. Usually any greasy spoon would do. When it was Kerouac's turn, he chose Phil's for its great steaks grilled in garlic butter. But Phil's was along US 1, much closer to Miami than to St. Pete. It took a great deal of poking, prodding, urging, and mocking for Kerouac to get his way. Finally, the bandmates pointed their Cadillac land cruiser south, and another road adventure was born.

It seemed fitting that Ron and I were sitting at a Denny's talking about all this. From his briefcase, Lowe pulled out a promotional picture of his band circa 1965. There were a few postcards and letters from Kerouac and a couple of autographed books. It was common for Kerouac to pull books off his shelf, sign them, and give them to friends as gifts. One of the books was a signed paperback copy of *Desolation Angels.* Lowe thinks Kerouac gave him the books "as a way of validating me for later—to write about him." One night, Ron Lowe brought up the subject of children. Kerouac "got pissed" and replied, "My books are my children. And my books will be on library shelves when your children's children's children are dust."

During this period, the impending publication of *Desolation Angels* helped pull Kerouac out of his depression over Caroline's death. In his so-called "Legend of Duluoz," *Desolation Angels* filled in the years 1956–1958, certainly among the most eventful of his life. "I look forward with glee to your reading it," Kerouac wrote his old friend Philip Whalen. "I especially want you to dig the beginning, about Desolation Peak." Kerouac was glad for the peaceful surroundings in Florida. "I can run my typewriter in the middle of the night without fear of someone peeking in the window," he reported to Whalen. "I've got to keep busy with my Legend or die of boredom."

A month after his forty-third birthday in March 1965, Kerouac gave Sterling Lord a status report on what had become of his book manuscripts. Kerouac still had the *Dharma Bums* and *Big Sur* teletype rolls with him in St. Petersburg. Others, including *Mexico City Blues*, *Tristessa, Desolation Angels, Doctor Sax, Book of Dreams,* and *Visions of Gerard,* were also at the house. Kerouac wrote some of his manuscripts in tiny pocket notebooks in a script so small that it almost takes a magnifying glass to decipher the words. With very few editorial changes, some of those little pocket notebooks Kerouac's friends and neighbors often referred to became the books seen on store shelves today.

Some of the reviews for *Desolation Angels* were positive. Encouraged, Kerouac revived a plan to travel to France to research his family roots. He also swore off hard liquor and spent the spring doing push-ups and headstands, or so he said. "Am all set for an interesting new concept," Kerouac told Sterling Lord, "of living without all that dreary repetitious muggle-headed bibulosity."

Once Kerouac received the $1,000 royalty check for *Desolation Angels,* he planned to go "winging to Paris." Besides the Paris research, Kerouac planned to spend part of the summer living along a canal in Amsterdam. The trip might also include a junket to England. Before his departure in May of 1965, Kerouac confided to Lord, "I've been very happy lately."

The trip lasted just two weeks, mainly because Kerouac reunited with an old flame—cognac. Writing from home on June 11, Kerouac insinuated to his agent that he had spent a great deal of time in bars. He also recounted an episode that seemed significant to him. Along the Seine River, Kerouac had entered the church of Saint Louis en l'Ile. Wet and disheveled from a rainstorm, Kerouac put his hat upside down in his lap to let the water run off. Apparently moved by his sad appearance, a family had dropped twenty centimes—equivalent to a handful of pennies—into Kerouac's hat.

The trip gave Kerouac enough stories for him to turn it into a new novel. From July 10 to 17, Kerouac wrote a 30,000-word account called *Satori in Paris.* During his seven-day writing blitz, to recapture the mood of his adventure, Kerouac drank a river of cognac. When finished, Kerouac hesitated to send *Satori* to his agent, feeling it was too short.

In the end, Kerouac felt the Europe trip really hadn't paid off. He was still struggling to make the mortgage and pay the bills. "I wish I hadn't gone to France at all," Kerouac wrote, "and saved that money to live on and just hang on."

Kerouac had remembered his neighbor Nell Burrow on that trip to France. Nell recalled the French cigarettes she'd received as a souvenir from Jack. Nell's daughter, Cheryl, also has a couple of Kerouac souvenirs, though not from the France trip. Jack and Memere gave a toy organ to Cheryl when she was a little girl. Kerouac used to like to create tunes on the little keyboard. She also has a tattered drawing by Kerouac. One day in 1965, Cheryl had brought over a picture of a cat she thought

Cheryl Burrow and the toy organ Kerouac gave to her when she was a child.

looked like Kerouac's. On the back, he began to doodle a picture for her. Under the cherished pine tree in his front yard, Kerouac completed the picture—a crucifix image with the inscription INRI. He added goblins and ghosts all around it. In the corner of the drawing, he signed his given name, Jean Louis Lebris de Kerouac. It was very rare for Kerouac to sign his given name to something he wrote or drew.

Kerouac and Memere also formed a friendship with another neighbor and her daughters. Betty Whatley lived a block away from the Kerouacs. Because the Kerouacs didn't own a car, Whatley often gave them rides. She visited the Kerouacs once or twice a week. On any given day Whatley would find Memere humming over her pots of simmering French food while Kerouac, wearing comfortable pants and a v-neck T-shirt, watched TV, listened to music, or perhaps played the piano. Whatley also remembered the cats— "*always* cats around." When Whatley brought her three young daughters along, Stormy, Mona, and Jeannie infused some welcome life into the Kerouac home, where the shades were always pulled.

Within that gloomy realm, Kerouac spent long stretches in front of the television set, often jotting random thoughts in his notebooks:

*6:25 Channel 8 weather—that guy is from 'round Boston

*Hullabaloo dancers from a distance shaking their asses to a beat in sheath dresses they look like insects.

*Tell the truth it comes back at ya

*Lord forgive my eyes and especially me tongue

*There's a rumour of paranoia in the air

Despite the impression of neighbors like Betty Whatley, Ron Lowe argues that the Kerouac he knew was far from the puttering literary lion content to peer out the shades of his darkened lair. On nights and early mornings out and about, he was "just Jack." The anonymity allowed Kerouac to temporarily drop the yolk of fame and become more like any other forty-three-year-old carouser. He wasn't to be found at the fancier places, either. Lowe says Kerouac preferred to prowl the little beach cantinas. One of Kerouac's favorites was a little dive called the Shipdeck. Kerouac relished the fact that, according to Lowe, "most of his conversation mates never had any idea who he was." The Shipdeck was little more than a few tables and a mixture of tourists and fishermen looking for a some idle talk and a couple of belts while breathing the Gulf's salty spray.

Kerouac also discovered a place popular with University of South Florida students called the Wild Boar. One of Kerouac's rituals was "bumping bellies" with the Boar's owner—a big-bellied, round-faced, six-foot-three 230-pounder named Gerry Wagner. Upon spotting one another, the two men would race towards each other and literally collide stomach-to-stomach, finishing with a brotherly embrace. Kerouac could drink for days, and his young friends had to handle him in shifts. One patron of the Wild Boar described seeing Kerouac for the first time:

> Pot-bellied, badly in need of a shave, wearing a lumberjack shirt and overalls that looked two sizes too big . . . Only because of the black hair and the tragic beautiful dark lines of his face was there a resemblance to the picture on the book jacket.

When Kerouac did want people to know who he was, he would hang out at the Beaux Arts coffeehouse in Pinellas Park, about the closest thing to a New York-type cultural scene the Tampa Bay area had to offer. There Kerouac could rap with a variety of musicians, writers, and other artists. Lowe and his band had acoustic jams in the torchlit garden at the Beaux Arts. Kerouac would try to blend in with his harmonica or ukulele. "Though he never proved he could play either," Lowe said.

Kerouac's correspondence with old friends grew rarer. To composer David Amram, Kerouac explained, "so little to say in letters anymore, as one grows older." He signed the letter "Nutty Jack."

Kerouac's binges forced him to decline a trip to New York and an invitation to speak at Brown University, but such was the duality that was coming to define Kerouac's life. Even as some in the Bay area saw him as a sad, belly-bumping drunken lout, Ivy League professors were starting to consider his work important in the pantheon of American literature.

In September of 1965, Kerouac complained to John Clellon Holmes that he was burned out on associating with college kids. "Altho I can drink them all under the table," Kerouac bragged. "I'm through with talking to people younger than myself, I want to act my age and associate with people my age, people of my own interests and ability and experience."

But most of those people had their own lives. Allen Ginsberg was busy with his career, though he might not have visited Kerouac anyway because of Memere's disapproval. In addition, the Vietnam conflict was becoming a flashpoint, and many of Kerouac's old associates, including Allen Ginsberg, embraced the antiwar movement. Kerouac abhorred politics and felt Ginsberg and the others were posturing. That meant more isolation. "I haven't got much left in the world," Kerouac admitted to Holmes, "but a few old friends like you."

Now that college students knew about Kerouac and where he lived, the inevitable ensued. He complained that some of them broke bottles in the street in front of his home. Others threw rocks at the door in the middle of the night. Kerouac blamed one such incident for causing one of his cats to run away.

Her peace destroyed, Memere wanted to move to Cape Cod. With a $2,200 check from foreign royalties in the bank, the dutiful son agreed to look for a new house in Hyannis, Massachusetts. Kerouac told Sterling Lord that they no longer had any reason to be in Florida, claiming, "We came here just to be near my sister anyway." Once again Kerouac blew what little money he had on a down payment and moving expenses.

The move took place in April of 1966. Ron Lowe would have been a natural to drive Kerouac and Memere to their new home in Hyannis, but he and his bandmates were on the road. So the job fell to Betty Whatley. She borrowed a friend's Chrysler New Yorker for the trip.

Kerouac took his place up front, while Memere and the three caged cats rode in the back. The next couple of days took them through a circuitous route to Massachusetts. Whatley recalled making one stop "right in the middle of Georgia, in the middle of nowhere," at a backwoods liquor store, where Kerouac and Memere augmented their cognac supply. The rest of the way, Memere serenaded the front-seat passengers with old French songs, nipping at her flask all the while. Memere always told her son, "I don't care what anybody says, a little drink never hurt nobody!"

Kerouac admired his mother's pragmatism. "The only thing to do," Kerouac wrote, "is be like my mother: patient, believing, careful, bleak, self-protective, glad for little favors, suspicious of great favors, make it in your own way, hurt no one, mind your own business, and make your compact with God."

The move to Hyannis set the stage for the crucial events of Kerouac's later life. He would eventually return to St. Petersburg, but not before events had changed his life forever.

An inscribed book from Kerouac to his neighbors Nell and Tex Burrow.

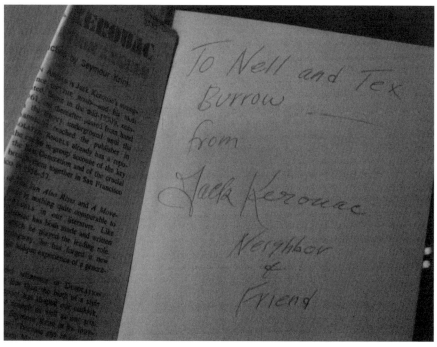

The Last Road Trip
1968

There she lies with her kittens and Stella slaves and
I do nothing but drink and think.

Jack Kerouac

Ron Lowe and the band were back from a road trip and playing a gig at the Captain's Lounge in St. Pete. In the midst of their set, a stocky man came in and proceeded to argue with the doorman about why he didn't have to pay the cover charge. *He* was friends with the band leader. The man flung up his arm and gave Lowe a hearty wave. Jack Kerouac was back in St. Petersburg. But this time the circumstances were much different, and Kerouac had brought someone new with him.

Kerouac had spent most of 1966 in Hyannis, Massachusetts, and had moved back to his hometown of Lowell in 1967. It had been a difficult and eventful time for Kerouac and his mother. Still grieving over Caroline's death, Memere suffered a debilitating stroke in September of 1966 that left her bedridden. Kerouac was forced to become his mother's caregiver. He bought rubber sheets and pillows to make her comfortable. He devised a way to put his head under his mother's armpit and lift her, "like in a wrestler's hold." For the first time in his life, Kerouac was confronted with the gravity of that promise he'd made to his dying father. Now he was truly taking care of Memere.

Kerouac's notebooks make it clear that his mother's disability deeply frightened him. Kerouac wrote prayers to God and Gerard, Mary and Jesus, that his mother would be able to get up and putter around the house on her own. Failing that, Kerouac faced the trying task of caring for an invalid mother himself, unless he could put her in a nursing home or get someone to care for her at home. For an answer, Jack Kerouac turned to an old friend.

Stella Sampas was the sister of Kerouac's cherished friend Sebastian Sampas, who died young in World War II. Less than five years after Kerouac wrote Stella that he was a confirmed bachelor, he proposed to her. Family members believe Stella had been carrying a torch for Kerouac ever since the days when he used to visit the Sampas family home at the bottom of Stevens Street in Lowell.

Kerouac seemed definitive when he wrote to Stella that he loved her "like a sister." However, when it was finally her turn, Stella became Kerouac's third wife. The wedding at Kerouac's Hyannis home on November 19, 1966, was simple and unadorned. The couple were married by a judge wearing tennis shorts.

Stella was marrying into a myriad of problems. Clearly the husband she had waited for all these years was now a hopeless alcoholic. Her disabled mother-in-law not only required constant care but openly resented anyone who tried to take her place with her son. Nevertheless, Stella willingly assumed the role of nursemaid and caretaker for Memere.

In February of 1968, Kerouac suffered an unexpected loss when Neal Cassady died in Mexico. Drugs and alcohol contributed to Neal's collapse as he was walking alone down a train track. Carolyn Cassady called Jack and Stella to break the news. At the time, Carolyn didn't know what had caused Neal's death, and Jack couldn't believe that Neal was really gone.

Another unexpected event of 1968 for Kerouac was seeing his daughter for the second and what turned out to be the last time. A teen-aged Jan stopped by her father's house in Lowell and found him sitting about a foot from the television set watching *The Beverly Hillbillies*. He was cradling a bottle of Jack Daniels "like a giant baby bottle." In the middle of Jan's visit, Memere awoke thinking Jan's voice was that of her daughter. She wheeled into the room screaming "like a bat out of hell," but Stella just walked in and wheeled her back out. Jan was headed for

Mexico, and on her way out, Kerouac told her if she wrote a book down there, she could use his name.

Kerouac felt that his life had taken a dreary turn. "I'm so busy and drunk too all the time, and befuddled," he confided to Ed White. Though he recognized that he was often out of control, he resented Stella's attempts to take charge. On one occasion, Stella was so upset at Jack's mounting phone bills that she tore up his address book. He made her piece it back together and then write a new one.

In the autumn of 1968, Memere told her son she couldn't stand another cold New England winter. She thought warmth might help her paralysis. "I know if I get in that Florida sunshine I'll get better," she promised. Kerouac obliged, perhaps not foreseeing that the move would leave him lonelier and more alienated than ever.

Kerouac insisted that the job of driving himself, Stella, and Memere back to Florida fall to his new road buddy—a friendly, hardworking, salt-of-the-earth Lowell native named Joe Chaput (pronounced sha-poo). On a road trip in 1967, Chaput had driven Kerouac to Canada.

When moving day came, Chaput and Kerouac fixed up a bunk in the back of a station wagon so Memere could lie down. As always, Stella attended to her mother-in-law. Kerouac rode shotgun with Chaput, who told him, "You're the navigator. One of your duties is to keep the pilot awake." To provide some help driving, another friend, Red Doherty, also came along.

On a scratchy old tape recording made before his death, Chaput recounted how Kerouac was up to the task of regaling all the passengers. Kerouac alternated between playing the harmonica and swilling scotch and malt liquor. He could talk for hours at a time as long as he had his little bottle with him. Once in a while Stella or his mother would chime in from the back, "Shut up. We're tired of hearing you talk." They'd obviously heard Kerouac spin these yarns for years. But for Joe and Red, the stories were new and entertaining.

Red took the wheel of the Lincoln Mercury wagon and zoomed through New York and New Jersey. Then, as Red "took a big snoring nap," Joe drove. The round-robin continued nonstop to Florida. A truck full of the Kerouacs' furniture, driven by friend Jim Dumphy, followed a few hours behind. On this day in early November, Kerouac had his last look at the exquisite colors of autumn in New England. More important-ly, it was the last time Kerouac was one with what always beckoned—life on the road. Just repeat his name—*Jack Kerouac, Jack Kerouac*—and you hear the sounds of his beloved roadbound life: fast cars flying down a long, black stretch of pavement in a wide-open expanse of land, hipsters in gas-guzzling jalopies looking for kicks that post–World War II, middle-class life couldn't often provide, the rhythm of motion, the pulse of opti-mism and adventure.

The travelers soon arrived safely in Florida. "We made Lowell to St. Petersburg in less than 24 hours, 1600 miles or so," Kerouac wrote Tony Sampas. "We were stopped for speeding in South Carolina but when the cop saw Memere and the cats and Stella in the back he just told us to pull over to a station and have our rear red warning lights refurbished." Kerouac helped the other men unload furniture and ended up putting a bad gash in his shinbone. Bloodied leg and all, that first night Kerouac enjoyed a bucket of Kentucky Fried Chicken for dinner.

Kerouac rented a motel suite for Joe and Red. "We went out and played pool and drank by the Gulf of Mexico waves at the Red Barn Club," Kerouac wrote. The Red Barn featured live music from the band-stand, and Kerouac hit the dance floor. "I jumped in the air, doing my Russian ballet entrechat, and kicked myself right in the nerve that runs along the shin."

The next day, the men went to see a doctor about getting the cut on Kerouac's leg patched up and getting a wheelchair for Memere. It was warm in the waiting room, and Jack's banged-up appearance drew a few stares. After about an hour and a half of waiting, Kerouac had had enough. "I cured myself my own way," he reported to Tony Sampas. "Saved a hundred or so for booze."

Back home, as hard as he tried, Kerouac couldn't get any of his old St. Pete buddies on the phone. "He couldn't locate a single person," Chaput recalled. "He was on the phone for an hour. Nobody was around."

That sense of sadness carried over to Joe Chaput's last day in St.

Petersburg. In the morning, Joe and Jack saw a French film in a nearly empty theater. After a few drinks, it was time for Chaput and the others to head back north. "It was an emotional goodbye with Jack. I wondered if I'd see him again, but he promised we'd get together in the spring."

On November 15, Kerouac sat down and wrote Chaput a letter about the new house in St. Petersburg. "Anyway Joe, we made our move real good and you ought to see how nice this house and neighborhood is coming out. It's sleepy time down South, everybody ben sleepin, includin me, since you and Red and Dumphy left." Kerouac had set up a bedroom office with access to the backyard. "I can step out this very second into the moonlight piney tree night," he told Chaput. "It's easy to talk happy like this when you're all happy and settled." Kerouac thanked Chaput for his help and called Joe his "A #1 man."

Two years after she had made *her* road trip with the Kerouacs, Betty Whatley opened her door to find Jack Kerouac standing there in a drunken stupor. He told her he had bought "Tex's house." His new place was right next door to the Kerouacs' last St. Petersburg home. He wanted Whatley to come over and meet his new wife. Betty and Stella would soon become friends, and Betty would be a great help to her neighbors during the trying times ahead.

When Kerouac had lived in St. Petersburg in 1964, he had admired the house next door where Tex and Nell Burrow lived. Tex had built his wife's dream house there on the corner of Tenth Avenue. They'd paneled the family room and closets in cedar they'd cut in the country, and Kerouac used to enjoy the way it smelled. But now Tex and Nell Burrow were splitting up. From Lowell, Kerouac had negotiated by phone the deal to buy the home, agreeing to a purchase price of more than fifty thousand dollars. Kerouac again saddled himself with a stiff mortgage at a time when his work was not selling well.

After his second move to St. Petersburg, Kerouac was quite a sight in his neighborhood. Shop owners recalled the jowly, red-eyed hobo plodding past to the liquor store, wearing a lumberjack shirt and unpressed pants. An architect neighbor recalled Kerouac sometimes coming over to use the phone. With a beer in one hand and a tumbler of scotch in the other, ranting about some conspiracy, Kerouac came off as "a little frightening."

"I used to worry over him as much as I did my own son," Nell Burrow recalled in a motherly tone. "I used to tell him *Jack, you drink all the time.*" He replied with a sly grin and a flash of his "big ol' blue eyes."

In that time period, hard-drinking men like Kerouac were hardly ever seen as diseased and in need of help. Performers like Dean Martin and Foster Brooks even made being drunk part of their act. The Kerouacs were like countless American families who suffered the disease in silence.

To protect himself from snoops and interlopers, most of them imagined, Kerouac had a five-foot fence erected, similar to the one he had built in Kingswood Manor. He used income from foreign royalties to pay for the construction, but his bills were mounting.

About this time Kerouac heard a rumor that his editor at Viking, Keith Jennison, planned to donate Kerouac's original *On the Road* scroll to a library. On December 3, 1968, Kerouac wrote a letter in protest. "It's my personal property, also my *concrete* physical property in that it's my paper and my ink and no one else's," Kerouac informed Jennison. "I'll be needing this to tide me over middle age in a very surprisingly unlucky literary career, from the financial standpoint."

Kerouac's paranoia crept into the letter. "Since I'm being blackballed by the new 'cultural' underground, I am certainly not going to give them the T-shirt off my back too." Kerouac managed to have the scroll delivered to his agent's office. It remained in Sterling Lord's safe for years, but that would not end the controversy over Kerouac's priceless first draft of what many consider to be his masterpiece.

When Kerouac met back up with Lowe, Stella had no reason to believe this youngster was any different from others tempting him to resume his carousing. She even took to hiding Kerouac's shoes. Kerouac solved the problem by having his young friends carry a pair of shoes his size in the car with them. Lowe kept a shoe ad Kerouac sent him, along with "9 and a half" written in the margin. Kerouac pulled the ruse on his wife like a giggling adolescent sneaking out of his parents' home at night.

Knowing that her husband's notebooks and manuscripts might be their key to long-term financial security and Kerouac's literary legacy, Stella was ever vigilant of them. Although Kerouac was meticulous in his record-keeping, he had the habit of pulling books off his shelf and presenting them as gifts to friends. That's how Lowe said he ended up with Kerouac's review copy of *Vanity of Duluoz*. However, when Stella found out Lowe had the book, she wrote him a polite postcard asking for it back. When Lowe tried to return the book, Kerouac asked indignantly, "What's this?" After hearing his friend's explanation, Kerouac made one of his trademark throat-clearing noises of disgust and amended some instructions he'd hand-written in the book. Where Kerouac had written "file copy lay off this book," he added "except for Ronnie Lowe."

To stave off increasing isolation and loneliness, Kerouac took to making late-night phone calls to old friends. John Clellon Holmes was one of those who got used to the phone ringing at all hours. "He used to call me up and say *damn it, get on the plane and come down!* I couldn't do it. I had my own life," Holmes recounted. "And yet I should have heard the desperate note in his voice."

Allen Ginsberg described the late-night, long and bittersweet phone conversations. Some, he said, were punctuated with vicious anti-Semitic slurs. But Ginsberg felt Kerouac was just doing that to get his goat.

Composer David Amram also took Kerouac's phone calls. Amram makes a case against Kerouac's being a true anti-Semite: "All the time I spent with Jack I never got one second of that [anti-Semitism] from him." In the early morning hours, Amram sometimes serenaded Kerouac through the phone line.

Carolyn Cassady remained Kerouac's lifeline to Neal's golden ghost. He often phoned up drunk, wanting to reflect on the good old days. Most times he refused to believe Neal was dead. Another time he told Carolyn, "Ah Neal, I'll be joining him soon."

Neal's son, John (Kerouac's godson), sometimes took those calls in the wee hours. "He would call at 3 A.M. drunk and rumble and rave, my mom trying to politely get him off the phone. I answered one night and only vaguely remember him crying *Johnny!* and *I have to speak to Carolyn!*

I handed her the phone and she looked worried."

On Easter morning of 1969, at six or seven o'clock Florida time, Carolyn's phone rang. Only this time she too had a head swimming from too much drink, and she didn't have the endurance for a marathon session with Kerouac. His voice was "mellow, slurred and cozy, ready for a nice, long chat." Ready for the comfort of her bed, Carolyn told him she'd be happy to chat later in the day, then hung up.

The phone rang again. Steeled with the determination and anger that come from being roused from sleep with a heavy head, Carolyn "pulled the pillow over [her] ears and gritted [her] teeth. Oh Jack, dear Jack, have mercy—*please* understand."

He never called again.

Most of Jack Kerouac's long-term friendships had eroded into disjointed late-night phone conversations or sorrowfully sad cards and letters based on perceptions and impressions from years past. Kerouac treasured Neal and Carolyn Cassady, but he saw them only a few times in the last ten years of his life. From looking at photos of him during that time, it's as if someone hit fast-forward on the aging process. Few wanted to be around to witness the train wreck that was Jack Kerouac's final years.

Kerouac's last home in St. Petersburg, next door to Kerouac's previous residence in 1964-65.

Jack's 47th

Jack Kerouac loved baseball so much he devised his own league using cards he created. For decades Kerouac had it all in his mind: eight fictional teams, dozens of imaginary ball players, and a 154-game season. There was El Negro of the St. Louis Whites. Wino Love anchored the Detroit Reds. Big Bill Louis was a crowd pleaser and everybody's favorite. Kerouac's imaginary center fielder, Sonny Sims, was modeled after Willie Mays. Another player, Pic Jackson, would be the inspiration for Kerouac's last novel, titled simply *Pic.* All of them competed for the pennant in the mind of one man. A flip of the card determined balls or strikes, hits or outs. Each batter had a hitting percentage, RBI's, home runs, doubles, triples and the like. Each pitcher had his own E.R.A. All the game statistics went into the official league stenographic notebook.

In February 1969, Kerouac was returning to St. Petersburg from a short trip to New York. On the airplane he befriended a young pitching prospect named John Warden from an expansion team, the Kansas City Royals. The next month, Kerouac heard Warden would be on the mound during a spring training game at Al Lang Stadium in downtown St. Petersburg. Kerouac decided to go watch, as he had watched Paul Gleason in Orlando. That's where Kerouac spent his forty-seventh birthday, March 12, 1969, with Ron Lowe.

At Lang Stadium, Kerouac bellowed encouragement to his young pal—so much so that an older couple close by gave up their seats and moved in an attempt to spare their ringing ears. Kerouac was oblivious. If that umpire was going to make calls against the kid, Kerouac was going to let everyone know about it. Despite all the encouragement, the young prospect was roughed up pretty well by opposing batters. After a couple of innings the manager pulled him. "He'll have another chance," Kerouac observed with optimism. "He's young."

That disappointment already behind him, Kerouac decided the next order of birthday business was a cold one. On this day that meant a double-decker ice-cream cone at Webb City, billed as "the world's most unusual drugstore," located at Ninth Street and First Avenue South.

It had been two decades since Kerouac blazed across country with Neal Cassady. The Beats had been replaced by hippies. And in 1969, America had a strange new road adventure to digest. Kerouac and Lowe pulled into the Mustang drive-in to check out Dennis Hopper's *Easy Rider*. The irony of it all was not lost on Lowe. "Imagine watching the late-sixties version of two guys on a wild ride across America with the man who'd redefined American literature with the publication of *On the Road*."

In view of how much Kerouac had changed, it's not surprising he gave a thumbs-down to the hippie classic. Kerouac asserted that he and Neal had celebrated America and had a good time. The characters created by Peter Fonda and Dennis Hopper acted out a drug-hazy road adventure punctuated by a violent denouement. Kerouac dismissed the film with a throat-clearing sound of disgust, followed by a wave of the hand. "They're trying to make heroes of those guys, and they're not heroes," Kerouac insisted. "They're criminals." Kerouac was no criminal, but he was no stranger to jails either, and Neal Cassady was hardly a choirboy. The hippie movement is forever tied to one of its foremost and yet recalcitrant architects, Jack Kerouac.

Ron Lowe and his bandmates were one of the few influences still around to pull Kerouac out of the protective confines of the home on Tenth Avenue. By 1969, the walls of his home were insulating, his constant alcohol intake debilitating. But on one particular late night, as Ron Lowe describes it, Kerouac gave a few flashes of the old days. Kerouac combed his hair, wore a white shirt with no tie, and a sport coat—all of this a drastic departure from his usual disheveled self. In Lowe's words, "Jack looked sharp." The two men and another buddy were off to catch a band at a Clearwater nightspot. There they met some ladies whose charm, according to Lowe, "was their availability."

One thing led to another, and soon the fivesome was back at Lowe's St. Pete pad on 22nd Avenue South. Finally, the wine and drink reduced Kerouac to the point where, Lowe says, "the boxcars had started to hit each other." As Kerouac continued in his ramble-snooze-then-ramble-some-more mode, he finally came to and realized that he was all alone.

And so it went for Kerouac in the town he nicknamed *Salt Petersburg*.

The Rosary
1969

How fitting then that this child of bliss should come in the end to Saint Petersburg. Our city of golden sunshine, balmy serenity and careless bliss, a paradise for those who have known hard times. And, at once, the city of wretched loneliness, the city of rootless wanderers, the city where so many come to die.

Roy Peter Clark

As the year 1969 continued, it brought both triumph and tragedy to America. Actress Judy Garland was found dead in England. Astronauts Neil Armstrong and Buzz Aldrin walked on the surface of the moon. Woodstock became the pinnacle of the peace and love movement. Amidst all of these events, Jack Kerouac learned that his liver was breaking down. Years of alcoholic excesses had caught up with him.

Kerouac had a "gray, stubbly, tragic old man's face," according to writer Richard Hill in an account of his visit with the remnants of "Ti Jean." But once in a while, the old flame inside Kerouac would flicker. When he would read aloud from his books, he made wild, sweeping gestures and used the grins, scowls, and posturings of a true thespian. One of Kerouac's drinking buddies and a reporter for the *St. Petersburg Times,* Jack McClintock, described Kerouac's expressive power: "The voice would go along, swoop up high, drop confidently low. It sped, it dragged portentously. It understood words and brought them alive."

These periodic moments of grace were overshadowed by the physical and mental changes in Kerouac. The chiseled features had given way to the rounded jowls of excessive drink. Kerouac's intellect was often muddled in a haze of obsessive thoughts about Communist conspiracies. Those around him during this time were subjected to a caricature of the handsome writer portrayed on the dust cover of his books.

On September 4, 1969, Kerouac ambled into lawyer Tom Bryson's office. Drunk and disheveled, Kerouac had to prove who he was. He fished a copy of *On the Road* from the Publix grocery bag he'd been carrying. "I want to make a will," he then declared to the bewildered lawyer. In terms of monetary value at the time, Kerouac didn't have much to leave. He had $3,900 in a savings account, and the sale of his Hyannis property had brought in another $4,300. All the assets, including the notebooks, letters, and manuscripts, were to go to Memere should he die before her.

Kerouac also made money from a syndicated magazine article he wrote called "Après Moi, le Deluge." This piece was Kerouac's testimonial about his position as a bridge between the Beats and the hippies. Kerouac referred to himself as a "Bippie-in-the-Middle." He made it clear that he did not share the antiwar politics of the hippies. Writing to David Amram, Kerouac expressed his opinion that the whole antiwar movement had become a "cottage industry" for those looking to turn a buck. According to Amram, "Jack's only politics were being an American."

On September 12, an article on Kerouac by Jack McClintock appeared in the *St. Petersburg Times.* The article illuminated Kerouac's decline as he passed day after day in the dimly lit living room, sipping scotch from a little pill vial, his sips punctuated by a "snap of the cap." "I'm glad to see you," Kerouac told his interviewer plaintively, "'cause I'm very lonely here."

Kerouac had a mind to do something about his loneliness. He sent a postcard to brother-in-law Nick Sampas about possibly returning to Lowell to start a newspaper. That idea suited Stella, for she was growing tired of the young crowd who came by and treated her husband's faded fame like some sideshow attraction. "Leeches, hangers-on, the worst," she called them. Memere, however, vetoed the idea. Winter was coming, and she couldn't bear the cold. Kerouac agreed to wait until the spring of

1970 to set his plan in motion.

At the beginning of October, despite the decline in his health and spirit, Kerouac finished his last novel. Stella and Betty Whatley helped Kerouac type his manuscript for *Pic*, the story of a ten-year-old black boy's journeys with his brother Slim, told in Southern country dialect. Kerouac had actually begun the story just after finishing *On the Road*, and he now considered writing a scene in which the brothers are picked up on the road by Dean Moriarty and Sal Paradise. But Stella argued that he couldn't just bring in characters from another book, so he trashed a handful of pages in frustration before the novel was completed. *Pic* brought in about $2,000, a welcome addition to the family's meager income from Stella's sewing jobs.

One of the rare times Kerouac ventured out that year, he brought home a manger scene he'd found behind a store somewhere. Kerouac's love for Christmas never died. "There it was October," Stella remembered, "and Jack was talking about putting out the manger."

Most of the time, Kerouac called his closest friends rather than leave his home in a drunken state. David Amram reflected on the last of Kerouac's rambling late-night phone calls to him. Previous calls had been joyous and entertaining. The two friends had talked about old friends and baseball and about musical interests like Chuck Berry, Little Richard, or Screamin' Jay Hawkins. Sometimes Kerouac would sing by himself, and sometimes the two would sing scat duets. But that last time, Kerouac had a cough and told Amram, "I'm not good." It was heartbreaking for Amram, who had an intuition that "he might be coming to the end."

In an autobiographical sketch written in 1960, Kerouac had described his vision of his last days: "Hermitage in the woods, quiet writing of old age, mellow hopes of Paradise (which comes to everybody anyway)." Perhaps *Paradise* was a tip of the hat to his alter ego from *On the Road*, Sal Paradise. However, Kerouac's dream of old age would never come true.

Early on the morning of October 20, Kerouac did some work on a project he had recently started. Entitled *Spotlight*, the book would continue

Kerouac's life story into the years of his fame. It would start by depicting Kerouac and Memere living in the Orlando back-porch apartment in the weeks before *On the Road*'s publication, when they were so broke that they argued about having dessert when they couldn't even afford meat for dinner.

Also on that October morning, Kerouac wrote a letter to Paul Blake Jr. informing him of the new will. Kerouac spelled out to Paul Jr. that his father should not think he would be able to get his hands on any of Kerouac's estate. The blood still ran cold from Caroline's death. Kerouac also spoke bitterly of divorcing Stella or having the marriage annulled. He didn't want her Greek relatives getting their hands on his things, though he had been willing to have *their* financial support. So, "just for the bloodline of it," Kerouac wanted to leave something to his nephew. It could also be that taking care of Paul Jr. was Kerouac's way to purge some of his own guilt about his relationship with his sister at the time she died. In the letter, Kerouac translated some words from Memere: "I'm very proud of you, my little blond boy, because you work for your country." Paul Jr., now twenty-one, was serving as an airman in Alaska. This letter was the last Kerouac ever wrote, and he never got a chance to mail it.

Later that day, Ron Lowe got a call from Kerouac, who told him he was throwing up blood. Kerouac blamed his sickness on some "goddamned tuna fish" he'd eaten. Within an hour, Lowe received another call. It was Stella, who said that Kerouac had been taken by ambulance to St. Anthony's Hospital. Lowe made it over to be with them. Betty Whatley was there, too.

Medical staff in the emergency room had no idea whose life they were being asked to save. When Kerouac was unloaded from the ambulance, he was coughing up an alarming amount of blood. Midge Laughlin, a chemist at the hospital, was asked to draw blood. "To be honest, I didn't know Jack Kerouac from a hole in the ground," Laughlin said in a later interview. "But I knew he was extremely critical." At the time she said she had trouble believing he was only forty-seven. "He looked terrible. I thought he was much older."

Inside Emergency, nurse Anne Houston had the impossible task of trying to replace all the blood Kerouac was losing. Many years later she remembered "racing from one side of the bed to the other, hanging unit after unit of blood." The hospital went through thirty units, which is almost four gallons of blood. Kerouac's liver had shut down, and he was bleeding into his chest and lungs. With all the blood loss, Houston said that the room "looked like a battlefield."

Ron Lowe recalled a doctor in a short-sleeved yellow dress shirt and collegiate striped tie thrusting his hands into a pan of alcohol. Kerouac's blood pressure was so low that the doctor didn't dare to put him under. Without anesthetic, the emergency team tried to insert a tube into Kerouac's throat to control the bleeding. A member of the team asked Lowe to come in and help restrain Kerouac, who was thrashing violently, slipping in and out of consciousness, screaming and swearing. Despite Lowe's considerable size, he had to apply a great deal of force to Kerouac's chest to control the violent movements. Even in his delirium, Kerouac kept trying to sit up. At one point, his eyes focused on his young friend, and he pleaded, "They're trying to kill me. Why are you helping them?" That was hardly the case, of course. Ron Lowe still has the card that shows he donated blood that day for Kerouac.

Kerouac was wheeled into surgery early on the morning of Tuesday, October 21. Stella was not allowed to stay with him. Anne Houston, Kerouac's nurse, was exhausted. Her last glimpse of Kerouac, the great American writer, was of him lying on his back headed for surgery. "It was horrible," she recounted sadly. "It was one of those situations where you didn't know how he could possibly make it." His death came as no surprise. Houston would find out only later whom the world had lost. After all this time, she is still saddened by the trauma he must have suffered.

Jack Kerouac died at 5:15 A.M. in the recovery room, with no family or friends present. For hours, the surgery team had worked fruitlessly to tie off the burst abdominal veins that let Kerouac's blood seep away. One of his surgeons later commented, "The poor guy was in shock from the time he hit the emergency room, and we never really got him out of shock."

That night, Walter Cronkite announced the news on CBS: "Jack Kerouac, the novelist who wrote *On the Road*, reached the end of it today. . . . Kerouac's books, selling millions of copies, translated into eighteen languages, were regarded as a bridge between older bohemian movements and today's hippies."

Kerouac's buddy during the last road trip from Lowell, Joe Chaput, said he heard the news at work in Lowell. *Jack Kerouac, the famous Lowell writer, died last night in St. Petersburg.* In a measured, matter-of-fact voice, Chaput recalled his reaction: "I was dumbstruck. I could barely keep the tears from flowing."

On October 22, *The New York Times* ran a two-column obituary, including a picture of a pensive Kerouac in his trademark plaid shirt. The *Times* noted, "Mr. Kerouac's admirers regarded him as a major literary innovator . . . this estimate of his achievement never gained wide acceptance among literary tastemakers." In the obituary Stella said that Kerouac had been drinking heavily for the last few days of his life and that "he was a very lonely man."

In a sad little procession, newly-widowed Stella Kerouac made her way down Tenth Avenue in a handmade black dress. By her side was the hulking young rock-and-roller Ron Lowe, pushing Memere in her wheelchair. They were headed to Kerouac's wake at the John Rhodes Funeral Home down on the corner. It was the same "red neoned funeral parlor" Kerouac had mentioned to John Clellon Holmes days after Caroline's death. Memere's beloved and last surviving child gone, she muttered sadly in French and English. She told Ron Lowe, "Jackie loved you. When you are here, I feel he is nearer."

Several weeks before his death, Kerouac had asked Lowe to take a rosary and $15 down to St. Jude's Catholic Church. He wanted Father O'Brien to bless the religious ornament for Memere. For a long time, the rosary had remained in an envelope in Lowe's car. Every time Lowe thought to do the favor for Kerouac, he was miles from the church. A buddy asked him, "Why don't you just pocket the $15, put it in your gas tank, and tell him you got the rosary blessed?"

Now Ron Lowe looked at his deceased friend. He thought Kerouac looked pretty good, all dressed up in a white shirt, bow tie, and checked houndstooth jacket. Lowe watched as Memere, with her one good arm, slipped a picture of Ronnie and his bandmates into Kerouac's jacket pocket.

Then Lowe recognized the rosary. The clear beads and crucifix were draped between Kerouac's folded, lifeless hands. The feeling hit Lowe like a blow to his chest. He hadn't pocketed the $15, and he was never more glad of anything in his life.

When the time came to take Kerouac's body back home to Lowell for burial, Stella didn't have the money and had to borrow it from one of her brothers. At first, Stella had thought it might be best to bury Kerouac with his other family in Nashua, New Hampshire. But her brothers convinced her to bury her husband in the Sampas family plot in Lowell. He would be next to his beloved wartime friend, Sebastian Sampas. Stella relented, saying, "He loved Sammy, and Sammy loved him." In a postcard Kerouac had written to Stella seventeen years after her brother's death, Kerouac ended the note with "I still miss Sammy."

* * * * * *

On a darkened stretch of Florida highway, the aging poet meditated. Along other stretches, Allen Ginsberg had whiled away the miles playing his harmonium, caressing the small squeeze box with a dexterity that impressed his youthful driver, writer Mark Burrell; but now he was quiet. The car streaked past the pitch-black rangelands, beneath the bleary eyes of truckers blasting their way down the highway between Gainesville and St. Petersburg.

Finally, the two men arrived at the corner house on Tenth Avenue. It had been a dozen years since Allen Ginsberg had seen Stella Sampas. For years after Kerouac's death and then Memere's in 1973, Stella had remained in her home on Tenth Avenue. If nothing else, she had friends like Betty Whatley, and there Stella remained as caretaker of Kerouac's home and his memory.

Although Stella had had little contact with Allen Ginsberg, she and Ginsberg greeted each other warmly and got on like old friends. Stella showed Ginsberg Kerouac's old notebooks, some from the time when Kerouac wrote of Ginsberg and Neal Cassady.

In an article for the Rollins College *Sandspur,* Burrell described Stella's cathartic plea to Ginsberg. "Stella Kerouac became sad as she let go the story of watching Jack go down the slow, hard way alone." She simply wanted to know why nobody would *agree* with him, why nobody showed him any respect. Tears rolled down her face as she pointed out Kerouac's stuffed chair in the corner and said, "He sat in that chair for years, for YEARS, and drank himself to death."

When they finished talking, Ginsberg took her hand. Two of Kerouac's loyal friends silently shared their loss.

THE FLORIDA
LEGACY

The Kerouac House today.

Who Will Be Gatekeeper?

[My father] was a very special guy, who a lot of people loved
and revered, or at least idolized, but I didn't know him.

Jan Kerouac

For years after his death, Jack Kerouac's phone number remained listed in the St. Petersburg phone book. A couple of times I even called the
home on the corner of Tenth Avenue. I didn't know whom I expected to
reach—the phone just rang and rang. Someone must have wanted the
number listed even after all of the home's living residents were gone.

Kerouac's brother-in-law, John Sampas, helped clear up the mystery.
"It's what folks do in New England," he told me, to explain why Stella
never wanted the name or the phone listing changed. John himself continued to keep the phone number listed, for sentimental reasons perhaps.
I pressed him further. "Is there more to it than that?"

"Yes there is," he told me. "In a way, he's still alive. It appeals to me
very much."

When in St. Petersburg to conduct business over the years, John
Sampas has stayed in the home. Sometimes people have called and asked
for Kerouac. Some are serious. Some are kids who have no idea this writer they've read or heard about has been dead much longer than they've
been alive.

"I just tell them," Sampas said, "Jack's not here."

The business of tending to the mass of Kerouac's unpublished
manuscripts, letters, and journals has stayed with the Sampas family.
After Stella's death in 1990, John oversaw the publishing of *Book of Blues,*

a primer of Kerouac's poetry that includes the poem "Orlando Blues." Two volumes of his letters, and *The Portable Jack Kerouac* followed. In the late 1990s, a book of Kerouac's Buddhist writings, *Some of the Dharma*, was released. There are also a Kerouac CD-ROM and a spoken-word tribute album featuring many artists inspired by Kerouac. Jack Kerouac, his books, and his legend remain a multi-million-dollar industry.

Twenty-five years after her father died, Jan Kerouac filed suit to assume control of his estate. Sides were drawn between those who sympathized with her personal battle to be accepted as her father's daughter and those who thought she was being manipulated by opportunists. It looked as if the end of Kerouac's road through Florida would be a legal battle waged in a St. Petersburg courtroom. The lawyer representing the Sampas family interests was in College Park, less than a mile from Kerouac's old back-porch apartment on Clouser Avenue. But that trial never came.

At issue was the signature on Memere's will. Had it been forged so that Stella (and the Sampas family) would become the beneficiary of Kerouac's estate? It was the stuff of a television movie. Before he died, Kerouac named his mother the sole beneficiary of his estate and quite conspicuously left his wife and Jan Kerouac out of the picture. When Memere passed away four years later, Stella inherited everything.

At the time, the estate was hardly worth a second look in terms of value. But when Jan filed suit in 1994, the landscape had changed dramatically. A series of biographies had renewed interest in Kerouac, and his writing had a solid place in college classrooms across the country. Kerouac's romantic notions of America resonated loudly both at home and abroad, and his books had been translated into dozens of languages. Film director Francis Ford Coppola had talked about finally bringing *On the Road* to the big screen. Kerouac's original scroll of *On the Road*, seen as one of the treasured artifacts of American twentieth-century literature, was valued at more than a million dollars. The novel itself was selling more than 100,000 copies annually.

In a move that cost him any hope of getting a piece of the Kerouac fortune, Paul Blake Jr., Kerouac's other blood relative, sided with Jan against the Sampas family. On a visit to Memere soon after Kerouac's death, Paul had acquired his uncle's last letter, which expressed Kerouac's wish that the estate go to him when Memere died. During all the years since, Paul had felt he was entitled to at least some of the Kerouac estate.

Handwriting analysts were brought in to determine whether Memere's signature was a fake. Her mental state during those last years was also brought into question. One camp believed it perfectly proper for Memere to leave everything to Stella. The other found it hard to fathom. Wouldn't Memere honor the intent of her son's last letter on October 20, 1969? Wasn't the family bloodline important to her too?

The litigation meant anybody and everybody who knew the Kerouacs during those years in St. Petersburg could wind up on the witness list. One important witness was Betty Whatley, who had remained Stella's closest friend until the end. One afternoon she sat down with lawyers from both sides in the legal war for a two-hour sworn deposition. Whatley told the lawyers that she never saw Jan Kerouac come to the house in St. Petersburg after her father died. She also described the visit made by Paul Blake Jr. and his father soon after Kerouac died. Perhaps still blaming Paul Sr. for Caroline's death, Memere was icy. Things got worse when the Blakes seemed bent on trying to take some of Jack's note-books and personal effects. Stella had called the police to settle the matter. For four long years, Whatley told the lawyers, neither of Gabrielle Kerouac's grandchildren helped in her care or expressed any interest in her.

But Paul Blake Jr. said he never stopped loving his grandmother, and he believes she never stopped loving him. During some of those trying times for Stella and Memere, Blake was serving his country in the Vietnam War. If he was nowhere near his grandmother, the U.S. government had given him no choice; and when he returned, Paul had to sort through his feelings about losing his father, fighting in the war, and where to go in his life. Paul's personal uncertainties led to substance-abuse problems, and he spent some time in jail.

Memere may or may not have been aware of Paul Blake's problems in the early 1970s. At any rate, she may well have chosen to entrust her son's legacy to the woman who had taken such good care of her.

Nell Burrow, who had been the Kerouacs' neighbor in St. Petersburg, described the "immaculate" care Stella took of bedridden Memere. "She would rub her back, rub her feet." And even though Stella was a smaller woman than Memere, she still lifted Memere out of bed to help her go to the bathroom. She cooked and cleaned and labored at what had to be thankless, endless, miserable work. "Stella was like a prisoner in her own home," Burrow said. Burrow believed that Stella Sampas was absolutely entitled to what little she received from the Kerouac estate.

With few writing royalties coming in after Jack's death, Stella and Memere's existence was very meager financially. Perhaps that is one reason that Stella, in Whatley's words, "wore Jack's v-neck T-shirts almost until the day she died." After Memere's death, Stella took in her own mother and once again played nursemaid to an aged relative. It seemed that was her lot in life. For years, Stella Sampas watched people she loved die.

John Sampas explained that Stella remained bitter about the way critics treated her husband and his family. For example, an early biography claimed that Caroline Blake Kerouac committed suicide by shooting herself. That egregious factual error enraged Stella and Memere. Both were Catholics who considered suicide a mortal sin. For years, Stella refused writers access to Kerouac's trove of unpublished journals and manuscripts, and that isolation may have made her a few enemies in the literary world.

As sides were drawn in the battle over Kerouac's legacy, Jan accused many of her father's old friends of turning against her. "I wonder why would they suddenly be against Kerouac's only child," she wrote in an open letter to New York University after she was barred from speaking at a conference there about her father's work. She also called Allen Ginsberg, who was one of the panelists, "the worst sort of hypocrite."

With the acrimony at its height, Jan Kerouac petitioned the Lowell Cemetery commission to have her father's remains disinterred from the Sampas plot in Lowell and moved to the Kerouac family plot at St. Louis de Gonzague Cemetery in Nashua, New Hampshire. "I want to move my father's body to its rightful family plot," Jan told the *Lowell Sun.* One journalist saw an "irrefutable poignancy to an abandoned daughter's desperate claim to the dust of her dead father."

Those sympathetic to the Sampas family remembered that the heart and soul of many of Kerouac's books came from the smokestack shadows of Lowell, not Nashua. If Jan had a huge hole in her soul where her father should have been, it was hopeless to try to fill that void with the remains of a man who took off on her before her birth. Jan's request was denied.

In her legal action, Jan Kerouac took issue with the Sampas family for selling some of her father's personal effects. For example, actor Johnny Depp had paid $15,000 for Kerouac's old raincoat, $5,000 for a suitcase, $3,000 for a rain hat, $10,000 for a tweed coat, and $5,000 for a letter. To Jan, that was evidence the Sampases were parting out her father's legacy to the highest bidder. "Anything and everything they can put their hands on in the estate, they are selling," she said. In truth, Jan Kerouac and Paul Blake Jr. also sold Jack Kerouac memorabilia.

Jan wanted to put all of her father's personal items on display in a museum. But that would have been difficult. Kerouac moved so often that many of his valuable possessions were gone, like the old rolltop desk where he wrote so many of his manuscripts. It likely ended up in an Orlando dump back in the '60s.

In the end, the years of courtroom squabbles brought nothing good to any of those involved. It likely exacerbated Jan Kerouac's decline and eventually her death from severe kidney disease at the age of forty-four.

On October 4, 1999, three years after Jan Kerouac's death, her lawsuit against the Kerouac estate was dismissed. However, the legal remnants lingered for several more years. In 2003, the aging man Jack Kerouac once knew as "little Paul" was living out of his pickup truck on the streets of Sacramento. His life had fallen apart, and he had become one of the hobos his uncle might have met and written about. Blake continued to argue that he deserved a part of the Kerouac fortune. "My uncle would have thought this was a bunch of balderdash," Blake said. "He wouldn't want to see me living out of a truck."

In reality, someone did save Jack Kerouac's estate—his last wife, Stella. In 1973, had Blake or Jan Kerouac inherited Jack Kerouac's estate, it likely would have been parted out and sold off, and there would have been nothing left to debate. True, Kerouac seemed furious at Stella and the Sampas family in the last letter he ever wrote. But in 1962, Kerouac had expressed the same kind of acrimony toward the Blakes as a result of their long-running family feuds. Sadly for Jan, Kerouac never seemed to show much interest in her at all.

Jack Kerouac died in 1969, but the debate over how his estate is run and who should handle it has not ended. That controversy was rekindled in the spring of 2001, when John Sampas' nephew, Tony Sampas, and his family put up the *On the Road* scroll—the Beat Generation's holy grail—for public auction. "The scroll needs to go into the public," nephew Tony said. "We have a financial imperative. I have to settle an estate, and we have some bills." Some people were worried that the scroll would go to a private collector and be locked away.

On auction day, the scroll fetched $2.4 million, a record amount for a literary manuscript at that time—not bad for a groundbreaking work of art that publishers laughed at for six years. The purchaser was James Irsay, owner of the NFL's Indianapolis Colts. Fears that the scroll would be withheld from the public proved unfounded when the new owner sent the scroll on tour so that others could see and admire Kerouac's seminal work.

Should the Kerouac estate have taken better care of Jan? Does Paul Blake Jr. have some moral claim to the "Legend of Duluoz"? Did John Sampas mishandle some estate affairs early on? It is up to time and others to judge what kind of gatekeepers the Sampas family has been to the Duluoz legend.

Jan Kerouac's need for her father's acceptance never died. Ron Lowe was one who respected that need, and he eventually befriended Jan. Their acquaintance began in the early 1990s, when Lowe introduced Jan Kerouac to those assembled at a St. Petersburg literary symposium. That led to phone calls and further correspondence between the two. Lowe found her to be charming at times, a bit grating at others, and eccentric. She once sent him a Christmas ornament in an old tomato soup can. Not realizing it was a gift, he nearly chucked it in the trash. At other times, like her father, Jan would call Lowe in the wee hours of the morning, "just to hear a reassuring voice."

In Kerouac's archive, there is an exquisite picture of Jan taken two years before her death. She's wearing her brunette hair up. Shiny gold earrings contrast with a dark blouse. Her lower lip seems to jut out ever so slightly. The resemblance to her father is undeniable.

Jan Kerouac's remains were buried in Nashua, New Hampshire, in the Kerouac family plot. At last, she has a place alongside the others in Jack Kerouac's family, but nowhere near her father.

The Kerouac House

I've always been one of those who feel the vibrations of history, especially in seemingly unremarkable places. It's a kind of presence—even if the significant events are long since over and the person behind them dead and gone. That presence stirs in me the desire to dig out and polish the raw nuggets of history.

The little cottage on Clouser Avenue is one of those places. John Ney, who was renting the house when I first visited, died years back, and his wife, Carol, moved into an apartment not far from Kingswood Manor. She took with her that wondrous first edition of *On the Road*. In a conversation years after the first time we met, I asked Carol what she had done with the book. "Oh, I sold that a long time ago to pay some of the bills from when John died," she told me matter-of-factly. The well-kept old book that Rose McCray had given to Carol Ney fetched $18,000.

I was inspired to trace Kerouac's life in Florida by an old friend in Kansas City, John Griffin. I had just gotten back from visiting Hemingway's house in Key West. "I wish we had something like that here," I told John.

"You know Jack Kerouac lived in Orlando, don't you?" he replied.

That was in the winter of 1996. The previous year, Kerouac's estate had published his first book of letters, and the timing couldn't have been better. The last few letters were sent from 1219 Yates Street in College Park. The beginning of my road map had been provided by Kerouac's own hand. At this first stop on my journey, I met Eleanore Feller, who lived in the Blakes' old house on Yates Street.

In March 1997, after a subsequent year of research, I convinced editors of the *Orlando Sentinel* to publish a 3,000-word article I'd written to commemorate what would have been Kerouac's seventy-fifth birthday. I knew that his extensive Orlando connections, which I'd begun to unearth, would be news in our history-starved city. Just a few days after the piece ran, an enthusiastic stranger rang me up at the office. "What we could do is buy the house and have writers live there rent-free," he said enthusiastically. "Then we could give them a scholarship to travel and write on the road like Kerouac did."

"What a great idea," I told him. "But just one question—Who is this?"

That was my introduction to Marty Cummins, the owner of Chapters, a vintage bookstore and restaurant just a few blocks away from Kerouac's old apartment on Clouser Avenue. A man of perpetual motion and ideas, Cummins became the driving force behind what has come to be known as the Kerouac Project, its formal name being The Jack Kerouac Writers-in-Residence Project of Orlando. Cummins saw the house as an opportunity to "put Orlando on the international arts map." Because of Cummins' tireless enthusiasm, I willingly made the transition from detached writer-journalist tracing Kerouac's story to preservationist, bent on making sure the Clouser cottage would remain for generations to come.

From that first conversation, Cummins has been the champion, savior, cheerleader, chauffeur, travel agent, and patron saint of this grassroots effort. He also ruffled a few feathers with his efforts, but had it not been for Cummins' tireless promotion, the Kerouac Project would never have gotten off the ground or stayed in the air. Marty's wife, Jan, helped shoulder much of the load at the bookstore while Cummins recruited people to help make this vision a reality.

There were others instrumental in saving what had become a rat-infested fire hazard of a home. College Park residents Summer Rodman, her mother Gail Patronis, and Grace and Fred Hagedorn, all of whom have an undying appreciation for things historic, put up the good-faith money to help buy the home and give the old Clouser cottage a chance at transformation. In recent years, College Park has turned into a trendy neighborhood, where small, deteriorating wood-frame houses are torn down and replaced. Had these early benefactors not given their time and money, this historic home would have been lost.

When it came time to form the project's national board of advisors, one of Kerouac's old friends became an invaluable champion. David Amram had the vision to see what neither I nor any of the rest of us in Orlando could imagine. Not only would the writers' retreat fulfill a dream of Kerouac's, it would also give Amram a platform from which he could continue to debunk the tired, old Beatnik stereotypes. The only means Amram needed to achieve his goal was simply to be himself. Amram's enthusiasm for what we planned, his willingness to make repeated Orlando trips to help raise funds, his uncompromising inclusiveness and lack of pretense, gave us vital credibility and confidence. David Amram was a guiding light, and he would provide the firsthand knowledge of what the Beats were really about to a new generation discovering Kerouac's work and his central Florida legacy.

In the summer of 1998, the Kerouac Project held a small news conference at Cummins' bookstore. Amram brought along historian Douglas Brinkley and Stella Sampas' nephew, Jim Sampas. That night we gathered at a little place on the Wekiva River near my home. At Alexander's Restaurant, Amram discussed his myriad connections with Kerouac, and Brinkley talked about the daunting task of writing the next great Kerouac biography. There we were in a slice of old Florida, a place not much changed since Kerouac lived here decades ago. Strolling along the wooden walkway over the river, we spied a small alligator, its glowing eyes peering up from under the dock. To this day when my wife, Karen, and I recall that night, David Amram's flute serenade of that little gator makes us smile all over again. It's a memory made that much more special because Alexander's burned to the ground a year later.

That initial news conference brought a critical piece of publicity in *USA Today.* On an airplane, Cleveland entrepreneur Jeffrey Cole read a blurb about the Kerouac Project. A long-time devotee of Kerouac's writing, he called up Marty Cummins and asked, "What can I do to help?" Never one to shy away from someone's genuine goodwill gesture, Cummins told him, "We could use about $50,000." Within days Cole, who had come to love Kerouac's work while in college, sent Cummins a chunk of company stock that, when sold, added up to $52,000. Building on the initial seed money we collected, Cole's donation insured that the house was ours and that the first phase of transformation could take place. Kerouac's historic home would belong to those determined to save it as a cultural landmark. Members of the Kerouac Project signed the mortgage.

In that same year, City Lights Bookstore owner and distinguished Beat poet Lawrence Ferlinghetti made a short stop at the Kerouac House. Later, at a packed reading at nearby Rollins College, he made the wry observation, "I got to see the home where Jack lived and was miserable." The comment drew laughter from the crowd. It was true. Kerouac had

Bob Kealing and Lawrence Ferlinghetti outside the Kerouac House in Orlando.

an intense love-hate relationship with Florida. In Orlando, the cottage on Clouser where he "took a dozen cold baths a day sweating and dying" from the Florida heat was also the place where he became the father of the Beats with the publication of *On the Road* and where he wrote *The Dharma Bums.*

In November of 1998, Douglas Brinkley published a cover story in *The Atlantic Monthly* detailing his review of some of Kerouac's unpublished notebooks and writings. In another move important to our credibility, he invited members of the Kerouac Project to New York for a party at the famous Algonquin Hotel.

In the room where Dorothy Parker once held court over the Algonquin Roundtable, a most impressive group of people central to Kerouac's life gathered. Joyce Johnson read from the letters she and Kerouac exchanged during that watershed year of 1957. Kerouac's agent, Sterling Lord, shared reminiscences. Gatekeepers of the Kerouac legacy, John and Jim Sampas, no doubt basked in the glow of the growing respect Kerouac's work was receiving. Mr. and Mrs. John F. Kennedy, Jr., electrified the room with their elegance.

Significant figures from the Beat movement have embraced the Kerouac House as the kind of tribute he would have loved. In autumn of 1999 Carolyn Cassady traveled to Orlando from England for a Kerouac House benefit. After so many invitations from her old flame Jack Kerouac, after all the years, it was her first visit to Florida. In College Park, she regaled crowds about the two loves of her life—Neal and Jack. On a cool October night, Cassady and I sat under an oak tree and talked about the regrets she had over Neal's loss. To me it was obvious that despite the divorce, she never stopped loving him. Neal Cassady was no literary outlaw to her, but rather the husband she loved and the father of her children. Despite his numerous affairs and indiscretions, Carolyn told me, "I should have understood—that was just part of him." Later, on a sunny afternoon, I snapped some photos of Carolyn sitting on an inviting tree swing in front of the Kerouac house. Each time posing, Carolyn arched her back proudly, like the great beauty she once was—the radiance still evident.

Cassady's black-and-white, circa-1952 picture of Neal and Jack now graces my softcover edition of *On the Road.* But there were so many other images of Kerouac from those days that Cassady laments not recording. "I keep thinking of him jackknife diving into our pool," Cassady remembered. "And why didn't I take a picture of him when he was out there playing with the kids?"

Such reminiscences help define Kerouac as a person. To Carolyn Cassady, he was no Beat iconoclast, but the brilliant and strikingly handsome romantic writer she met more than a half century ago in the streets of Denver. He was the cherished friend who never found a comfortable transition into the later stages of life. As alcohol slowly destroyed Kerouac, Carolyn Cassady's voice at the other end of a phone line was one of the few comforts he found.

Ron Lowe and David Amram, along with other close friends of Kerouac, also made the trip to Orlando for the benefit. David Amram had come despite a recent devastating fire at his home in Peekskill Hollow, New York. For Ron Lowe, it was a night he would not soon forget. Despite having to make the long drive back to St. Pete, Lowe shared stories with Cassady and Amram until early in the morning.

At the time, Ron Lowe had gotten a contract to write a book about his experiences with Kerouac. He'd even settled on a title—*St. Jack: Kerouac in Exile.* This came as a victory for friends who for years had urged him to write down his memories. Lowe had vast experience writing articles for the *St. Petersburg Times,* and he had penned rousing political speeches. He had a column in the city's weekly African American newspaper with the tongue-in-cheek pen name I. B. White. Ron Lowe could write, and yet he confided in me that he never knew how to go about writing about his times with Kerouac. Early on he'd had a fear of exploiting those stories. They were loose and anecdotal, lacking cohesion, and the idea of structuring them into a book seemed to infect Ron Lowe with a case of terminal block.

On December 27, 2001, Ron Lowe died of pancreatitis at the Northside Hospital and Heart Institute of St. Petersburg. He was fifty-nine. I hope I related some of Lowe's stories half as well as he did. Now he and Jack are back on a roof somewhere, playing twelve-bar blues between bull sessions, and no doubt someone has already asked, "Who the hell is this new guy on bass?"

The year 2000 brought another of Kerouac's cohorts to Orlando—Steve Allen. In 1959 the television pioneer had the vision to put Jack Kerouac on his nationally televised show. Kerouac received $2,000, which he used to insulate the attic of his Northport home. Beyond helping pay the bills, the appearance was a wonderful showcase for Kerouac and his work. Because of that appearance, his work received national exposure and credibility, and we can see for eternity Jack Kerouac in Technicolor—before his great decline. Kerouac sat in a chair behind the piano, facing the camera, while Steve Allen laced a few jazzy licks. The pain of reading his work in public was plain on Kerouac's face, though, to me, it seemed that Allen was as nervous as Kerouac. But Kerouac performed with the confidence of believing the writing would be his legacy in this world. "And nobody, nobody knows what's going to happen to anybody, besides the forlorn *rags* of growing old," Kerouac snarled, reading from *On the Road.*

More than forty years after that special night with Jack Kerouac, Steve Allen had come to College Park to pay tribute to the man he said he loved. Upon meeting him, I could tell Allen was in ill health. Yet he talked nimbly with David Amram about the musicians and artists they had come to know over the years. Allen spoke of giving comedian Don Knotts his start. It was on this occasion that Allen met the first writer to be named a Jack Kerouac Project Writer-in-Residence—a young North Carolina poet named Erin Ann Styers.

Allen, Amram, and others piled into a long black limousine for the short drive over to the Kerouac House. Once inside, the group admired a 1939 Underwood typewriter just like the one Kerouac used to write *On the Road.* Allen reflected on the home's small confines and went into a short speech about how people in bygone days *were* physically smaller. But when he wound down and really took time to reflect upon Kerouac's time here, Steve Allen said, "It's something pretty special that's hard to put into words." I could tell how special it was for David Amram, too, who had not been together with Steve Allen since a 1956 fundraiser for Adlai Stevenson.

Doug Brinkley was also there. As he alternately talked and listened, I could almost hear the wheels turning in his mind, recording the moment for the biography he would write about Kerouac. During this visit, Brinkley called the Clouser house "the most important Jack Kerouac historical site in America outside of Lowell, Massachusetts."

That night in September 2000, for the first time ever, David Amram and Steve Allen appeared together on stage. Hundreds turned out in a banquet room at the Dubsdread Golf Course in College Park. It was a block from the apartment where Caroline Blake died, and another block from Edgewater Drive, the main artery through the heart of Kerouac's Orlando. It turned out to be the last public performance Steve Allen ever gave.

The evening was loose and unscripted. "Nothing has been planned. And if it has, it hasn't been brought to my attention." Allen's deadpan

The sign marking renovation of the Kerouac House in 2001.

brought laughter from the audience. Then he became serious. "I loved Jack Kerouac," Allen said sincerely. He went on to share his experience of reading a magazine excerpt of Kerouac's writing long before *On the Road* made Kerouac a national sensation. "One of the most beautiful examples of nature writing I'd ever encountered," he said. In tribute to the friendship he'd made a half century before, Steve Allen stood alone squinting in a spotlight and read from *On the Road.* David Amram provided the soft musical accompaniment, as he might have at the first jazz-poetry reading in New York with Kerouac in 1957.

The performance ended with a rousing rendition of the song Amram penned with Kerouac, "Pull My Daisy." Then Allen, Amram, and Brinkley sat together taking questions from the crowd. I thought about Allen's considerable legacy beyond his friendship with Kerouac. He had put Lenny Bruce on his show and defended the edgy comedian's biting social commentary. Allen had also had Elvis Presley come out in a tux and tails and sing "Hound Dog" to a bewildered-looking Bassett hound. He had written scores of books and songs and acted in movies. And he performed this last concert for free. For Jack.

Hours after the performance, sixty-nine-year-old Amram sat among friends at a Winter Park piano bar. We were just around the corner from where Kerouac landed at the bus station that first visit in 1956. As on other nights, Amram was the most energized of any of us. "What would Jack think of this, all these years later?" I asked Amram. "He would have cried," Amram said, without pausing a beat.

A loyal supporter of Kerouac and his legacy for years, Amram believes this is the kind of tribute Kerouac would have loved most. It's not about Kerouac the man, or the cautionary tale that was his life. It's not about with whom he went to bed or why he drank too much. "It's all about his writing and the enduring spirit of his work," Amram said. "And it's about what Kerouac's writing represents: honesty, inclusiveness, love for America, a yearning to be free from the restraints of conformity."

The little house Jack and Memere shared is now home to those who hope to be inspired by Kerouac's devotion to writing. Writers from all over the world live here for three-month intervals. The vibrations of those all-night typing sessions in 1957 and '58 today inspire work written from the Kerouac House.

Many of the artists who've passed through have commented on the value of their experience. "The oak trees pushing against the tin roof make a scratching sound," the first Kerouac writer-in-residence, Erin Styers, said, "not unlike that of a pencil to paper." Xu Xi, the second writer-in-residence, said the residency infused Kerouac's love of music into her work. "I would sometimes sleep with the radio on all night tuned to the jazz station," she wrote. "It seemed a fitting tribute to Kerouac's love of jazz." Another early writer-in-residence, Christine Markowski, said the stay influenced her decision to write full-time. "The turning point in my life was the day I entered that beautiful house with the fifties interior decorations," Markowski remembered. "I began to rediscover the poetry I buried when I was working in the world."

In 2001 the state of Florida approved a grant of $82,000 to help renovate and restore the Kerouac House. The award represented the first state money dedicated to the project. More importantly, it gave a crucial validation of the home's historic value and of Kerouac's importance as an American literary icon. The money allowed us to take that decrepit, cavelike cottage and transform it into a bright, inspiring place for a new generation of writers to work. Soon after the renovation was done, the transformation complete, a television crew helped us share our good news with the literary world.

"Sum it all up for me," C-Span producer Mark Farkas asked. "Put the importance of this house and Kerouac's life in Florida into perspective." The question was hard to get right. I needed to hand him the pages of this book, rather than try to put what I had learned into a two- or three-minute reply.

Farkas is the man behind C-Span's American Writers series, in which Jack Kerouac was going to be featured, and he had come to College Park for an in-depth story about Kerouac's Orlando connections. We'd gotten some attention from newspapers around the country, but this was the first time a national media outlet planned to include Orlando and the Clouser house in the tapestry of Kerouac's life.

I sat out front with the C-Span crew under the giant oak and answered questions. Then I showed the crew the sparkling gem that was once Carol and John Ney's cluttered cubbyhole and, before that, Jack Kerouac's refuge from fame. The room where Fred DeWitt photographed Kerouac now has his classic pictures on the wall. Kerouac's old writing room is freshly painted and has a new entry so one doesn't have to go through the bathroom to get there. The dark, wood-grain paneling has been replaced by bright colors and a terrazzo tile floor. However, I still have to duck when I come in the back way.

Next, in a little procession, we drove from College Park over to Kingswood Manor. Farkas and his partner, Paul, videotaped Kerouac's home on Alfred Drive. A large American flag hanging from one of Kerouac's cherished front-yard pines flapped softly in the breeze of the sunny afternoon. Ken Sears wasn't home.

Bob Kealing and the C-Span crew outside the Kerouac House.

I looked across the street at Audrey and Dave Redding's house. A neighbor came up and asked what the camera was for. I introduced myself and explained. When I asked about the Reddings, to my sad surprise the neighbor told me, "Dave Redding just died of a heart attack." It had been too long since I'd called or stopped by to see how the Reddings were getting along. I also found out that the Blakes' old home had burned down. The neighbor had bought the lot, renovated the burned shell, and connected his house to it. It's the kind of place the Kerouacs and Blakes might have built if the Sanlando Springs dream had ever come true.

Our last stop was Greenwood Cemetery. We crunched fallen leaves underfoot as we made our way to Caroline and Paul Blake's grave. At the gravesite, among the shriveled maple leaves, I was surprised to see two small concrete squares marked with the letter B. "Maybe that's for the

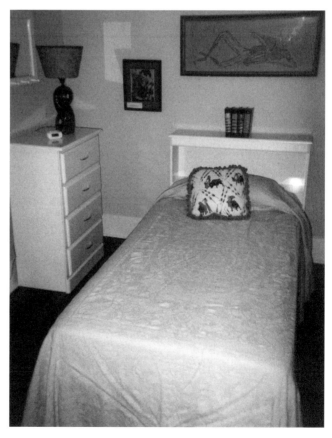

Kerouac's renovated writing room in the Clouser back-porch apartment, where he wrote *The Dharma Bums.*

Blakes," we surmised. Those simple markers must have been added since the first time I visited.

In 2003 James Irsay agreed to bring Kerouac's *On the Road* manuscript to Orlando for a three-month exhibition at the Orange County Regional History Center. The scroll that brought Kerouac years of rejection before it brought him fame was returning to Orlando as the literary treasure it has become.

On a recent outing at the Wekiva golf course near my home, I stepped off the eleventh tee to do what you sometimes have to during the course of a four-hour round. Obscured amidst a small stand of scrub pines, vines, and palmettos was a gorgeous tree ripe with Florida oranges—a remnant from the days when this whole area teemed with groves. Being from the Midwest, I still regard this kind of discovery as wondrous. And I'm proud to say the Kerouac House on Clouser Avenue was the same kind of discovery, a hidden Florida jewel. The last step in polishing that jewel is complete. Kerouac's vision of a writing retreat in Florida has come true, and Orlando residents, hungry to claim something historic that pre-dates Disney, can call this their own.

More than once, Jack Kerouac's road ended here in Florida. Now we can see Kerouac in a context that evokes memories of Florida's past: sleeping in a moonlit yard with the sweet aroma of orange trees all around, straining to hear the velvet whisper of the wind and his brother Gerard in the piney Orlando night, embarking on a sunrise hitchhiking journey along Orange Blossom Trail, returning with his rucksack full of manuscripts and dreams, watching *Sputnik* shoot across the stars, injecting excitement into the bar scene in a lonely city by the Gulf. No one can say Kerouac only came to Florida to die.

As we move further beyond the twentieth century, it is inevitable that more of our history will be written in suburban post–World War II America. The tract houses and manicured lawns give a false impression that they are sterile and emotionless. The suburbs lack the pulse and vibrancy of cities, but people are the common denominator. Their lives share the same hopes, dreams, disappointments, tragedies, creativity, and love.

In his books, Jack Kerouac is forever the gentle, angelheaded romantic wanderer. In the end, not all of his life became literature. Kerouac's time in central Florida brought significant ruts in the road, and he did not have the chance to finish his life's work or to wear the "forlorn rags" of old age. But Jack Kerouac came to Florida and lived.

David Amram greets Carolyn Cassady outside the Kerouac House. Marty and Jan Cummins are also pictured.

Kerouac's Florida Time Line

December 1956	Arrives at the Winter Park, Florida, bus station
January 1957	Travels to New York City and meets Joyce Glassman (Johnson)
February 1957	Leaves New York City for Tangier, Morocco
May 1957	Returns to Orlando, Florida, long enough to pack for move to Berkeley, California
July 1957	Moves back to Orlando and rents Clouser apartment
September 1957	Travels to New York City for publication of *On the Road*
October 1957	Returns to Orlando
November–December 1957	Writes *The Dharma Bums* in the Clouser apartment
April 1958	Moves to Northport, New York
August 1959	Abandons plan to build communal home in Sanlando Springs, Florida
May 1961	Moves to Orlando, 1309 Alfred Drive in Kingswood Manor
October 1961	Writes *Big Sur* in the Alfred Drive, home
December 1962	Moves to Northport, New York

September 1964	Moves to St. Petersburg, 5155 Tenth Avenue
September 19, 1964	Caroline Kerouac Blake dies in Orlando
May 1965	Travels to Paris to research family roots
July 1965	Writes *Satori in Paris* in the Tenth Avenue home
April 1966	Moves to Hyannis, Massachusetts
November 19, 1966	Marries Stella Sampas
January 1967	Moves to Lowell, Massachusetts
November 1968	Moves back to St. Petersburg, 5169 Tenth Avenue
October 21, 1969	Dies at St. Anthony's Hospital, St. Petersburg

Notes

Introduction

5   "I have another novel": Jack Kerouac notebook entry, 7-24-48. Berg Collection.

6   "What man most wishes to hide": JK to Malcolm Cowley, 9-11-55. Berg Collection.

6   "Neal and I are in Mexico City": JK notebook entry, 1949. Berg Collection.

7   "To a critic": JK notebook dated 1965. Berg Collection.

8   "It's raining": JK to Sebastian Sampas, March 1944. Berg Collection.

Yates Street

11   "So therefore I dedicate myself to myself": JK's letter to himself, 9-5-45. Berg Collection.

11   "Hello, over here": Author's conversation with Eleanore Feller, February 1996.

12   *The Town and the City* was published by Harcourt Brace in 1950. However, Harcourt rejected Kerouac's next submission, *On the Road.*

12   Million and a half words: In a notebook, Kerouac tallied each work by number of words and came up with this figure. Berg Collection.

12 "the honest record": Malcolm Cowley, quoted in Jack Kerouac, *Selected Letters, 1940–1956,* ed. Ann Charters (New York: Viking Penguin, 1995), p. 597.

13 Stillborn twin: Author's conversation with Paul Blake Jr., 1-29-97.

13 "On the porch": JK, *Desolation Angels* (New York: Penguin Putnam, 1995), p. 319.

14 "You'd be talking": John J. Dorfner, *Visions of Rocky Mount* (Raleigh: Cooper Street Publishers, 1991).

14 "obscene burlesque dance": Jacksonville Judge Marion Gooding, quoted in *Orlando Sentinel Star,* 8-11-56.

15 "parties of people": JK, "Not Long Ago Joy Abounded at Christmas," *Good Blonde and Others* (San Francisco: Grey Fox, 1993, 1994), p. 101.

15 "sweetheart": JK to Helen Weaver, December 1956. Courtesy of Ken Lopez.

15 "what I'd do to you": Ibid.

16 "It is the DEFINITE road of beatness": JK to Keith Jennison, 12-26-56. Berg Collection.

16 "Tho I'm supposed to be": JK to Helen Weaver, 1-5-57, in Jack Kerouac, *Selected Letters, 1957–1969,* ed. Ann Charters (New York: Viking Penguin, 1996), p. 3.

16 "He totally charmed me": Joyce Johnson, "Fresh Air with Terry Gross," produced in Philadelphia by WHYY, 6-15-01.

17 "I'm praying now": JK to Neal Cassady, 3-25-57, *Selected Letters, 1957–1969,* p. 21.

17 "I sure do hope": Ibid.

17 "There's hardly anything": JK, *Desolation Angels,* pp. 377–78.

17 "It's hot in May in Florida": Ibid., p. 377.

18 "towards the panhandle": Ibid., p. 378.

18 "Sometimes during the night": Ibid.

18 "little ole earth quake": Ibid., p. 407.

18 "California is sinister": Ibid., p. 394.

18   "He never brought her down here": Carolyn Cassady, *Off the Road* (New York: William Morrow, 1990), p. 289.

18   "I remember and realize": JK letter to Snyder, 6-24-57, *Selected Letters, 1957–1969*, p. 44.

19   "You know, he lived": Author's conversation with Eleanore Feller, February 1996.

1418 ¹/₂ Clouser Avenue

20   "And this is the way": Kerouac notebook entry, 1948. Berg Collection.

20   "It says here": Author's conversation with John Sampas, March 1996.

21   "I'll never move again": Memere quoted in JK letter to Malcolm Cowley, 7-21-57, *Selected Letters, 1957–1969*, p. 53.

21   "heatwave horror": JK to Ginsberg et al., 7-21-57, *Selected Letters, 1957–1969*, p. 54.

21   "complete solitude": JK to Cowley, 7-21-57, *Selected Letters, 1957–1969*, p. 53.

21   "God knows": Ibid.

21   "I feel the call": Ibid.

22   "Everybody comes around every night to laugh": JK to Joyce Glassman, 7-22-57, *Selected Letters, 1957–1969*, p. 56.

22   "In a year": Ibid.

22   "I GOT ASIATIC FLU": JK to Ginsberg, 8-9-57, *Selected Letters, 1957–1969*, p. 59.

22   "I just couldn't sweat it out": JK to Glassman, 8-18-57, *Selected Letters, 1957–1969*, p. 61.

22   "He had absolutely no notion": Johnson, "Fresh Air with Terry Gross."

23   "an authentic work of art": Millstein, *The New York Times*, 9-5-57.

23   "He could barely": Johnson, "Fresh Air with Terry Gross."

23   "drunk alatime": Cassady, *Off the Road*, p. 290.

24	"Neal and I, too": Ibid.
24	"I can't think of any": Johnson, "Fresh Air with Terry Gross."
24	"The only way": Ibid.
25	"I found myself": Ibid.
26	"I slept & slept": JK to Glassman, 10-14-57. Berg Collection.
26	"These next five years": Joyce Johnson, *Door Wide Open* (New York: Viking Penguin, 2000), p. 78.
26	"It became apparent": Johnson, "Fresh Air with Terry Gross."
27	"On this machine": JK to Glassman, 11-1-57. Berg Collection.
27	"I was wondering": JK to Neal Cassady, late October 1957. Berg Collection.
28	"I've got to make Dharma Bums great": Kerouac 1957 notebook. Berg Collection.
28	"a brown star": Ibid.
28	"If Viking": Ibid.
28	"not as dramatic": Ibid.
28	"packs explosive significance": Ibid.
28	"Oh well": Ibid.
28	"This poor kid": JK, *The Dharma Bums* (New York: Viking, 1958), Chapter 10.
29	"What wouldn't I have given": Kerouac notebook dated 12-8-57. Berg Collection.
29	"I don't wanta get married": JK to Glassman, 12-17-57. Berg Collection.
29	"I laced a few jazz licks": Author's conversation with Steve Allen, September 2000.
29	"Broke up with Joyce": JK to Ginsberg, 12-28-57. Berg Collection.

A Good Neighbor

Quotations in this chapter are from the author's conversation with John and Carol Ney, March 1996.

Fred's Photos

34   "Aren't you the guy": Author's conversation with Bob Eginton, July 2001.

35   Kerouac wrote about his 1958 trip with Robert Frank in the story "On the Road to Florida," *Good Blonde and Others.*

35   "I pulled up alongside here": Author's conversation with Fred DeWitt, August 2001.

35   "He was waiting": Ibid.

37   "I know you can't see it": Fred DeWitt at Joe Brooks' photo lab, March 2002.

37   "tawdry and slapdash": *Time* magazine review, 2-24-58. J. Paul Getty appears on the cover.

37   "I remember going back": Author's conversation with Fred Dewitt, August 2001.

37   "It's OK": Ibid.

39   "a dozen cold baths": JK, *Desolation Angels,* p. 407.

44   "In reality": Author's conversation with John Sampas, October 2003.

Sanlando Springs

45   "As for <u>me</u>": JK notebook entry dated 7-28-48. Berg Collection.

46   "When I write in my yard": JK to Caroline Kerouac Blake, late May, 1959. Berg Collection.

46   "big emergency telegrams": Ibid.

46   "There's alot of traveling": JK to Caroline Kerouac Blake, 1-29-59. Berg Collection.

46   "This is important": Ibid.

46   "It would be cute": Ibid.

47   "I have a 3000 dollar": JK to Caroline Kerouac Blake, late May, 1959.

47   "It may come in handy": Memere to Caroline Kerouac Blake, 1-29-59. Berg Collection.

48   "My Ma prefers": JK to Donald Allen, 10-1-59. Berg Collection.

48   Paul Blake sold it: Author's conversation with Paul Blake Jr., 1-29-97.

Kingswood Manor

50   "There's a noise in the void": Jack Kerouac notebook dated February 1950. Berg Collection.

50   "Jack Kerouac was my neighbor": Author's conversation with Audrey Redding, 6-27-96.

51   "My mother and brother": Ibid.

51   Jackie Kennedy reference: JK *Selected Letters, 1957–1969,* p. 271.

52   "It was great": JK to Sterling Lord, 5-5-61. Berg Collection.

53   Duluoz Legend: John Sampas explained to the author that Kerouac picked the name *Duluoz* at random out of the *Lowell Sun.*

53   "It was kind of low-key": Author's conversation with Audrey Redding, 6-27-96.

54   "It was nice till now": JK to Lois Sorrells, 5-31-61. Berg Collection.

54   "I'm quiet and happy": Ibid.

54   "Livingroom is too fancy": Ibid.

55   "Japanese TV redlamp": Ibid.

55   "Across the street": Kerouac notebook dated 1961. Berg Collection.

55   "I was really amazed": Author's conversation with Audrey Redding, 6-27-96.

55   "50,000 words": JK to Carolyn Cassady, 10-17-61. Berg Collection.

55   "I shoulda been an architect": JK to Ed White, 8-7-61. Courtesy of Ed White.

55   "feel just like dropping dead": Ibid.

56   "A bright fall will come": Ibid.

56   "You saw her in the door": JK, *Desolation Angels,* p. 317.

56   "Jack was asleep": Author's conversation with Audrey Redding, 6-27-96.

56   "A yellow cab would show up": Author's conversation with Dave Redding, 6-27-96.

57   "I dedicate myself to myself": JK's letter to himself, 9-5-45. Berg Collection.

57   "I'll never forget": Author's conversation with Audrey Redding, 6-27-96.

57   "I am going": JK to Ed White, 8-7-61. Courtesy of Ed White.

57   "Sposing the judge": Ibid.

57   "On your trip": JK to Lawrence Ferlinghetti, 8-28-61. Berg Collection.

58   "for the psychological blocks": JK to Sterling Lord, 10-9-61. Berg Collection.

58   "But O so sad": Ibid.

58   "I hope you appreciate": JK to Carolyn Cassady, 10-17-61. Berg Collection.

58   "But in years": Ibid.

58   "Got from a healthy tanned": JK to Philip Whalen, 10-17-61. Berg Collection.

59   "I've just finished": Ibid.

59   "What I'm actually doing": JK to Carolyn Cassady, 1-7-62. Berg Collection.

59   "I'm very happy": Ibid.

59   "I have a daughter": Jim Jones, *Use My Name: Jack Kerouac's Forgotten Families* (Toronto: ECW Press, 1999), p. 104.

59   "So that's my cousin?": Ibid.

59   "I am a hopeless": JK to Robert Giroux, 3-31-62. Berg Collection.

60   "You ought to go burn a cross": Gerald Nicosia, *Memory Babe* (Berkeley and Los Angeles: University of California Press, 1983), p. 634.

60   "almost" burned a cross: Author's conversation with Paul Blake Jr., 1-29-97.

60 "I ben drinking": JK to Lois Sorrells, 8-17-62. Berg Collection.

61 "I have to handle": JK to Stella Sampas, 11-17-62. Berg Collection.

61 "I have so much mail": JK to David Amram, July 1968. Courtesy of David Amram.

61 "looked beat": Author's conversation with Dave Redding, 6-27-96.

62 "Dad didn't want any bilingual": Author's conversation with Paul Blake Jr., 1-29-97.

62 "needless luxuries": Kerouac notebook entry dated October 1962. Kerouac Estate.

62 $1350 fee: Ibid.

62 "Togetherness America": JK to John Clellon Holmes, 10-16-64. Kerouac Estate.

62 "I just wanted to come over": Author's conversation with Audrey Redding, 6-27-96.

Jack and the Boys of Summer

Quotations in this chapter are from the author's conversation with Paul Gleason, June 2003.

Kenny's Discovery

69 "This was one fantastic thing": Author's conversation with Ken Sears, June 1996.

69 "Hippies would show up": Author's conversation with Ken Sears, 7-2-96.

69 "He finally sobered up": Ibid.

71 "Like a little boy": Jack McClintock, "This Is Where the Ride Ends, Not with a Bang, with a Damn Hernia," *Esquire,* March 1970.

71 "I'm always trying to think of a way": Sears, 7-2-96.

Locked in Grief

75 "The last time": JK to John Clellon Holmes, 10-16-64. Kerouac Estate.

75 "Mind you": JK and Memere to Caroline Kerouac Blake, 3-25-63. Berg Collection.

75 Money borrowed by Nin: JK letter to Caroline Blake, 1963. Berg Collection.

76 "Got escorted": JK to Philip Whalen, 11-18-63. Berg Collection.

76 Money problems reported by Ann Charters in JK *Selected Letters, 1957–1969*, p. 381.

76 "I lost some": JK to Sterling Lord, 9-9-64. Berg Collection.

76 "They didn't have": Author's conversation with Nell Burrow, 9-18-96.

77 "He'd always carry": Ibid.

77 Income mentioned in JK letter to John Clellon Holmes, 10-16-64. Kerouac Estate.

77 $5,000: Ibid.

77 Caroline called by police: Author's conversation with Audrey Redding, 6-27-96.

77 "One day": Ibid.

78 Caroline tried to sell furniture: Ibid.

78 14th Fairway Apartments: Author's conversation with Paul Blake Jr., 1-29-97.

78 Mowed lawns: Ibid.

78 "No one got divorced": Author's conversation with Charles Blackton, 7-13-96.

78 90 pounds: JK to John Clellon Holmes, 10-16-64. Kerouac Estate.

78 "If that's the way": Ibid.

78 Came back from getting sodas: Author's conversation with Paul Blake Jr., 1-29-97.

78 Details of Kerouac's finding out about his sister: JK *Selected Letters, 1957–1969*, p. 383.

78   Author's research at Berg Collection turned up no immediate notation of Caroline Kerouac's death.

79   Funeral details: *Orlando Sentinel Star* obituary, 9-21-64.

79   Kerouac locked himself in the bathroom: Author's conversation with Audrey Redding, 6-27-96.

79   Paul Blake Sr.'s conduct: Ibid.

79   "Yes, Paul": Author's conversation with Dave Redding, 6-27-96.

79   "abandoned and hopeless": Audrey Redding letter to author, 7-28-03.

79   "her husband left her": JK to John Clellon Holmes, 10-16-64. Kerouac Estate.

79   "loyal heart": Ibid.

79   "I gave her hell": Ibid.

80   "more mystified": Ibid.

80   Kerouac and the pine trees: Author's conversation with Nell Burrow, 9-18-96.

80   "First time in jail": JK to John Clellon Holmes, 12-8-64. Berg Collection.

For Nin

81   Caroline's military service: Author's conversation with Paul Blake Jr., 1-29-97. Florida death certificate for Caroline Blake.

81   City of Orlando: Online history of Greenwood Cemetery.

82   Caroline Blake's remains cremated: Author's conversation with Paul Blake Jr., 1-29-97.

82   Date of funeral: *Orlando Sentinel Star* obituary, 9-21-64.

82   Baptist preacher: Ibid.

83   "Nin hung": JK, "In the Ring," *Good Blonde and Others.*

83   "My father always planned": Author's conversation with Paul Blake Jr., 1-29-97.

83   Move to California and Paul Sr.'s death: Ibid.

85   "As I grew older": Kerouac, *Satori in Paris* (New York: Grove, 1965).

85   Lowe's band broke color barriers: Greg Williams, "Dominoes Band Leader Ron Lowe Dies at 59," *St. Petersburg Times*, 1-2-02.

85   "White in spots": Ibid.

86   Lowe meets Kerouac: Author's conversation with Ron Lowe, 5-18-96.

87   "C'mon in" Ibid.

87   "I don't mind" Ibid.

87   "the American mystic": Ron Lowe, "Jack Kerouac's St. Petersburg Sojourn," *St. Petersburg Times*, 6-7-92.

87   "Hemingway and Melville": Ibid.

89   "We fumed": JK, *On the Road* (New York: Penguin, 1991), p. 55.

89   "He instigated": Lowe, "Jack Kerouac's St. Petersburg Sojourn."

89   Phil's: Author's conversation with Lowe, 5-18-96.

89   "as a way of validating me": Ibid.

89   "My books are my children": Ibid.

89   "I look forward": JK to Philip Whalen, 1-10-65. Berg Collection.

90   "I can run my typewriter": Ibid.

90   "I've got to keep busy": Ibid.

90   Status report: JK to Sterling Lord, 4-16-65. Berg Collection.

90   "Am all set": Ibid.

90   "winging to Paris": JK to Sterling Lord, 5-8-65. Berg Collection.

90   "I've been very happy": Ibid.

90   Details of Europe trip and *Satori* writing efforts: JK *Selected Letters, 1957–1969*, pp. 402-403.

91   Money problems: JK to John Clellon Holmes, 7-21-65. Berg Collection.

91   "I wish I hadn't": JK to Sterling Lord, 8-2-65. Berg Collection.

91   Souvenirs from France: Author's conversation with Nell and Cheryl Burrow, 9-18-96.

92   "always cats": Author's conversation with Betty Whatley, 6-27-96.

92   1965 notebook entries: Berg Collection.

92   "just Jack": Author's conversation with Lowe, 5-18-96.

92   "most of his conversation mates": Ron Lowe, "Cruising the Old Haunts and Hangouts," *St. Petersburg Times*, 3-7-93.

93   Bumping bellies: Author's conversation with Lowe, 5-18-96.

93   Handle him in shifts: Larry Vickers, "Jack Kerouac: End of the Road," in Rudi Horemans, ed., *Beat Indeed* (Antwerp, Belgium: Exa, 1985), p. 33.

93   "Pot-bellied": Vickers, Ibid.

93   Kerouac at the Beaux Arts: Author's conversation with Lowe, 7-9-96.

93   "Though he never proved": Ibid.

93   "so little to say": JK to David Amram, 2-27-65. Provided by David Amram.

93   Brown invitation: JK to John Clellon Holmes, 9-18-65. Berg Collection.

93   "Altho I can drink": Ibid.

93   "I'm through": Ibid.

94   Kerouac despising politics and distancing himself from Ginsberg: Author's conversation with David Amram, 10-1-96.

94   "I haven't got much left": JK to John Clellon Holmes, 9-18-65. Berg Collection.

94   Breaking bottles in the street: Ibid.

94   Cat ran away: JK to Sterling Lord, 10-12-6. Berg Collection.

94   Royalty check: Ibid.

94   "We came here just": Ibid.

94   Driving the Kerouacs: Author's conversation with Betty Whatley, 6-27-96.

94   "Right in the middle of Georgia": Ibid.

94   "I don't care": JK, *Desolation Angels*, pp. 381-382.

95   "The only thing to do": Ibid, p. 380.

96   "There she lies": JK notebook dated 1966. Berg Collection.

96   Kerouac back in town: Author's conversation with Lowe, 5-18-96.

96   Details of Memere's stroke: JK to Stella Sampas, 10-12-66. Berg Collection.

96   "wrestler's hold": Ibid.

96   Prayers for his mother's recovery: Ibid.

97   Stella's love for Jack: Stella Sampas to JK and Gabrielle Kerouac, 7-21-66. Berg Collection.

97   "like a sister": JK to Stella, 10-12-66. Berg Collection.

97   Wedding date: Tom Clark, *Jack Kerouac: A Biography* (New York: Marlowe, 1984), pp. 203-204.

97   Judge in tennis shorts: Ibid.

97   Memere's resentment: Author's conversation with Nell Burrow, 9-18-96.

97   Details of Neal's death: Author's conversation with Carolyn Cassady, October 1999.

97   Jack couldn't believe: Ibid.

97   Jan's visit with Kerouac: Jan Kerouac, *Baby Driver* (New York: St. Martin's, 1981).

97   "giant baby bottle": Ibid.

98   "I'm so busy": JK letter to Ed White, 1968. Courtesy of Ed White.

98   Stella tore up Jack's address book: Author's conversation with Ed White, 8-2-96.

98   "I know if I get": JK to Ed White, November 1968. Recounted by Ed White.

98   "You're the navigator": Joe Chaput recorded memoir, provided by Phil Chaput.

98   "big snoring nap": JK to Tony Sampas, 12-5-68. Berg Collection.

99   Truck full of furniture: Ibid.

99   "We made Lowell": Ibid.

99   "We were stopped": Ibid.

99   "We went out": JK to Tony Sampas, 12-5-68. Berg Collection.

99   "I jumped": Ibid.

99   "I cured": Ibid.

99   "He couldn't locate": Joe Chaput recorded memoir, provided by Phil Chaput.

100   "It was an emotional": Ibid.

100   "Anyway Joe": JK to Joe Chaput, 11-15-68. Berg Collection.

100   Standing there in a drunken stupor: Author's conversation with Stormy Harper, 6-27-96.

100   Details of the house: Author's conversation with Nell Burrow, 9-18-96.

100   jowly, red-eyed hobo: Clark, *Jack Kerouac,* p. 214.

100   Lumberjack shirt and unpressed pants: Author's conversation with neighbor Jan Riner.

101   "A little frightening": Ibid.

101   "I used to worry": Author's conversation with Nell Burrow, 9-18-96.

101   "big ol' blue eyes": Ibid.

101   "It's my personal property": JK to Keith Jennison, 12-3-68. Berg Collection.

101   "Since I'm being": Ibid.

101   Years in the safe: JK *Selected Letters, 1957–1969,* p. 461.

101   Hiding his shoes: Author's conversation with Lowe, 5-18-96.

102   Stella's polite postcard: Ibid.

102   "file copy lay off this book": Ibid.

102   "He used to call me up": John Clellon Holmes, in Barry Gifford and Lawrence Lee, *Jack's Book,* (New York: St. Martin's, 1978), p. 311.

102   Get his goat: Ibid., p. 312.

102   "never got one second": Author's conversation with David Amram, 10-1-96.

102   "Ah Neal, I'll be joining him": Cassady, *Off the Road,* p. 422.

102   "He would call": Levi Asher, "Interview with John Cassady," Literary Kicks website.

103   Easter phone call: Cassady, *Off the Road,* p. 423.

103   "pulled the pillow": Ibid., p. 424.

Jack's 47th

104   Kerouac's baseball league: Stan Isaacs, "Playing 'Baseball' with Jack Kerouac," *Newsday,* 2-17-61.

104   Young KC Royals prospect: JK to Tony Sampas, 2-28-69. Berg Collection.

104   Kerouac at Al Lang Stadium: Lowe, "Cruising the Old Haunts and Hangouts."

105   "He'll have another chance": Ibid.

105   Ice-cream cone: Ibid.

105   "Imagine watching": Ibid.

105   "They're trying to make heroes": Ibid.

105   "Jack looked sharp": Author's conversation with Lowe, 7-9-96.

106   "The boxcars": Ibid.

106   "Salt Petersburg": Ibid.

The Rosary

107   "How fitting": Roy Peter Clark, *St. Petersburg Times,* 10-29-78.

107   Judy Garland died June 22, 1969.

107   Neil Armstrong walked on the moon July 20, 1969.

107   Woodstock festival, August 15-17, 1969.

107   "gray, stubbly, tragic old man's face": Richard Hill, "Jack Kerouac's Last Days," *St. Petersburg Times,* 10-21-87.

107   "The voice would swoop": McClintock, "This Is Where the Ride Ends."

108   "Communist conspiracies": Roy Peter Clark, *St. Petersburg Times,* 10-29-78.

108   "I want to make a will": William Levesque, "The Fight over All Things Kerouac," *St. Petersburg Times,* 11-24-02.

108   Value of the estate: "Kerouac Not Jack, But Jean," *St. Petersburg Evening Independent,* 10-25-69.

108   "All the assets": Last Will and Testament of Jean Kerouac, 9-4-69. Provided by the Kerouac Estate.

108   "cottage industry": Author's conversation with David Amram, 10-1-96.

108   "Jack's only politics": Ibid.

108   "Snap of the cap": McClintock, "This Is Where the Ride Ends."

108   "I'm glad": Ibid.

108   "Leeches": Interview with Stella Kerouac, 3-13-73, in Barry Gifford, *Kerouac's Town* (Berkeley, CA: Creative Arts, 1977).

108   Memere vetoed the move": Gifford and Lee, *Jack's Book,* p. 313.

109   Stella and Betty typed *Pic*: Author's conversation with Betty Whatley, 6-27-96.

109   Stella argued: Ibid.

109   Stella's sewing jobs: Ibid.

109   "There it was October": Gifford, *Kerouac's Town.*

109   Late-night phone call: Author's conversation with Amram, 10-1-96.

109   "Hermitage": JK, Introduction to *Lonesome Traveller* (New York: Grove, 1960).

109   *Spotlight* plot: detailed JK letter to Sterling Lord, 9-27-68. Berg Collection.

110   Details of last letter: JK to Paul Blake Jr., 10-20-69. Provided by the Kerouac Estate.

110   "just for the bloodline": Ibid.

110   "I'm very proud": Ibid.

110   "goddamned tuna fish": Author's conversation with Lowe, 7-9-96.

110   "To be honest": Author's conversation with Midge Laughlin, May 1996.

111   "racing from one side": Author's interview with Anne Houston, 5-17-96.

111 Thirty units of blood: "Attempt to Save Life Depletes Blood Bank," *St. Petersburg Times*, 10-24-69.

111 "They're trying to kill me": Author's conversation with Lowe, 7-9-96.

111 "It was horrible": Author's interview with Houston, 5-17-96.

111 5:15 A.M.: Certificate of Death for John L. Kerouac. Provided by the Kerouac Estate.

111 Kerouac alone: Dudley Clendenin, "Jack Kerouac Dies Here at 47," *St. Petersburg Times*, 10-22-69.

111 "The poor guy": Ibid.

111 CBS Evening News with Walter Cronkite: 10-21-69.

112 "I was dumbstruck": Joe Chaput recorded memoir, provided by Phil Chaput.

112 "Mr. Kerouac's admirers": "Jack Kerouac, Novelist, Dead: Father of the Beat Generation," *The New York Times*, Joseph Lelyveld, 10-22-69.

112 "a very lonely man": Ibid.

112 Details of Kerouac's request to have the rosary blessed: Author's conversation with Lowe, 7-9-96.

113 Not enough money: Deposition of Elizabeth Whatley, 5-17-95. Case #73-4767-3E.

113 Stella decides on burying Kerouac in Lowell: Gifford, *Kerouac's Town*.

113 How he loved Sammy: Ibid.

113 "I still miss Sammy": JK to Stella Sampas, 7-29-59. Berg Collection.

113 Driving Ginsberg: Mark Burrell, "Roundabout Again," *Rollins College Sandspur*, October 1988.

113 Memere died on Thanksgiving Day, 1973: Gifford, *Kerouac's Town*.

114 "Stella Kerouac became sad": Burrell, "Roundabout Again."

114 "He sat in that chair for years": Ibid.

Who Will Be Gatekeeper?

117 "[My father] was a very special guy": Quoted in Jim Jones, *Use My Name*, pp. 134-35.

117 Kerouac's number, 813-321-3625, remained listed in the St. Petersburg phone book well into the late 1990s.

117 "It appeals to me": Author's conversation with John Sampas, July 1996.

118 Case #73-4767-3E, Jan Kerouac, Petitioner.

118 Stella inherited everything: Renee Tawa, "The Beat Battle Goes On and On," *Los Angeles Times*, 5-30-98.

118 In 2001 Christie's valued the scroll at between $1–1.5 million: *The New York Times*, 3-22-01.

118 More than 100,000 copies a year: Ibid.

119 Last Will and Testament of Jean Kerouac, 9-4-69.

119 Betty Whatley deposition, 5-17-95.

119 Details of Paul Blake Jr.'s life: Author's conversation with Paul Blake, 1-29-97.

120 Stella's "immaculate" care: Author's conversation with Nell Burrow, 9-18-96.

120 "wore Jack's v-neck T-shirts": Ibid.

120 Stella bitter: Author's conversation with John Sampas, July 1996.

120 The biography was by Ann Charters, who later admitted a "bad mistake" concerning Caroline Blake's death. Reported in Renee Tawa, "The Beat Battle Goes On and On," *Los Angeles Times*, 5-30-98.

120 "I wonder why": Jan Kerouac, "An Open Letter," June 1995, Literary Kicks website, Levi Asher.

120 "the worst sort": Ibid.

120 "I want to move my father's body": "Novelist Jan Kerouac 44," AP Obituary, 6-7-96.

121 "Irrefutable poignancy": Brian McGrory, "Penniless Kerouac Focus of Costly Court Fight," *The Boston Globe*, 5-29-94.

121 Depp and Kerouac's clothing: Levesque, "The Fight over All Things Kerouac," *St. Petersburg Times*, 11-24-02.

121 "Anything and everything": McGrory, "Penniless Kerouac Focus of Costly Court Fight."

121 Paul Blake Jr.'s life falling apart: Blair Robertson, "The Kerouac Connection," *Sacramento Bee*, 1-19-03.

121 "My uncle would have thought": Ibid.

122 In October 1962, Kerouac wrote in his notebook, "May God make me a millionaire someday so I won't lend or leave anything to any <u>Blakes</u>." Provided by the Kerouac Estate.

122 "The scroll needs to go into the public": Kathryn Shattuck, "Kerouac's Road Scroll Rolls Out to Auction," *The New York Times*, 3-22-01.

122 $2.4 million: "New York Library Buys Kerouac Archive," *The New York Times*, 8-22-01.

123 "Just to hear a reassuring voice": Author's conversation with Ron Lowe, 7-9-96.

123 Jan buried in Kerouac plot: Author's conversation with John Sampas, July 1996.

The Kerouac House

124 "Oh, I sold that": Author's conversation with Carol Ney, February 2002.

124 The book was Jack Kerouac, *Selected Letters, 1940-1956*, edited by Ann Charters.

124 Bob Kealing, "The Road to Kerouac," *Orlando Sentinel*, 3-9-97.

125 "What we could do": Author's conversation with Walter "Marty" Cummins, March 1997.

126 The Kerouac Project news conference took place in College Park, Florida, July 1998.

126 "What can I do?" Author's conversation with Marty Cummins.

127 "I got to see": Lawrence Ferlinghetti at Rollins College, October 1998.

128   "took a dozen cold baths": JK, *Desolation Angels*, p. 407.

129   The author was present at the event featuring Cassady, Amram, and Ron Lowe. Details of what happened late that night were provided by Amram and Marty Cummins.

129   Ron Lowe mentioned his book contract to the author.

129   Ron Lowe's death: Greg Williams, "Dominoes band leader Ron Lowe dies at 59," *St. Petersburg Times*, 1-2-02.

130    $2,000 for TV appearance: JK letter to Gary Snyder. Berg Collection.

130   "And nobody": JK, *On the Road*, p. 310.

130   "It's something pretty special": Author's conversation with Steve Allen, September 2000.

131   "the most important": Author's conversation with Doug Brinkley, September 2000.

133   "The oak trees": Erin Styers correspondence, 2001. Provided by Yvonne David.

133   "I would sometimes sleep": Xu Xi, Ibid.

133   "The turning point": Christine Markowski, Ibid.

133   "Sum it all up": Author's conversation with Mark Farkas, February 2002.

133   Kerouac was featured on C-Span's American Writers Series, 6-9-02.

137   Allen Ginsberg's poem *Howl*, published in 1956, describes the Beats as "angelheaded hipsters burning for the ancient heavenly connection to the starry dynamo in the machinery of night."

137   "Forlorn Rags": JK, *On the Road*, p. 310.

Selected Bibliography

Amram, David. *Offbeat: Collaborating with Kerouac.* New York: Thunder's Mouth, 2002.

Burroughs, William S. *The Letters of William S. Burroughs, 1945–1959.* Ed. Oliver Harris. New York: Penguin, 1993.

Cassady, Carolyn. *Off the Road: My Years with Cassady, Kerouac, and Ginsberg.* New York: William Morrow, 1990.

Clark, Tom. *Jack Kerouac: A Biography.* New York: Marlowe, 1984.

Gifford, Barry. *Kerouac's Town.* Berkeley, CA: Creative Arts, 1977.

Gifford, Barry, and Lawrence Lee. *Jack's Book: An Oral Biography of Jack Kerouac.* New York: St. Martin's, 1978.

Holmes, John Clellon. *Gone in October: Last Reflections on Jack Kerouac.* Boise: Limberlost, 1985.

Horemans, Rudi, ed. *Beat Indeed!* Antwerp, Belgium: Exa, 1985.

Johnson, Joyce. *Door Wide Open: A Beat Love Affair in Letters, 1957–1958.* New York: Penguin, 2000.

Johnson, Joyce. *Minor Characters.* New York: Doubleday, 1983.

Jones, Jim. *Use My Name: Jack Kerouac's Forgotten Families.* Toronto: ECW Press, 1999.

Kerouac, Jack. *Atop an Underwood: Early Stories and Other Writings.* Ed. Paul Marion. New York: Viking, 1999.

Kerouac, Jack. *Big Sur.* New York: Farrar, 1961.

Kerouac, Jack. *Desolation Angels.* New York: Berkeley, 1965.

Kerouac, Jack. *The Dharma Bums.* New York: Viking, 1958.

Kerouac, Jack. *Good Blonde and Others.* San Francisco: Grey Fox Press, 1993, 1994. John Sampas Literary Representative.

Kerouac, Jack. *On the Road.* New York: Viking, 1957.

Kerouac, Jack. *The Portable Jack Kerouac.* New York: Viking Penguin, 1995.

Kerouac, Jack. *Selected Letters, 1940–1956.* Ed. Ann Charters. New York: Viking Penguin, 1995.

Kerouac, Jack. *Selected Letters, 1957–1969.* Ed. Ann Charters. New York: Viking Penguin, 1999.

Kerouac, Jack. *The Town and the City.* New York: Harcourt Brace, 1950.

Kerouac, Jack. *Vanity of Duluoz.* New York: Coward-McCann, 1968.

Kerouac, Jan. *Baby Driver.* New York: St. Martin's, 1981.

McDermott, Mickey, with Howard Eisenberg. *A Funny Thing Happened on the Way to Cooperstown.* Chicago: Triumph Books, 2003.

Miles, Barry. *Jack Kerouac: King of the Beats.* New York: Holt, 1998.

Montgomery, John. *Kerouac at the "Wild Boar" and Other Skirmishes.* San Anselmo, CA: Fels and Firn, 1986.

Nicosia, Gerald. *Memory Babe: A Critical Biography of Jack Kerouac.* Berkeley and Los Angeles: U of California Press, 1983.

Index